INSECTS

Life Cycles and the Seasons

INSECTS

Life Cycles and the Seasons

JOHN BRACKENBURY

BLANDFORD

Paperback first published in the UK 1995
by Cassell plc
Wellington House
125 Strand
London WC2R 0BB

Distributed in the United States by Sterling Publishing Co., Inc.
387 Park Avenue South, New York, NY 10016–8810

Distributed in Australia by Capricorn Link (Australia) Pty Ltd
2/13 Carrington Road, Castle Hill, NSW 2154

British Library Cataloguing-in-Publication Data
A catalogue entry for this title is available from the British Library

ISBN 0-7137-2598-2

Typeset by Cambrian Typesetters, Frimley, Surrey

Printed and bound in Hong Kong
by
Dah Hua Printing Co. Ltd.

CONTENTS

INTRODUCTION

I RECALL WITH some pleasure the day when I first found a hibernating queen hornet wasp, curled up inside the chamber that it had excavated for itself under the bark of a dead tree. It was February and the weather was bitterly cold. There had been continuous frosts for three weeks. The sight of this beautiful, colourful insect riding out the winter on a mere pulse of life was strangely engrossing. At the time, it seemed a million miles from the image of the same insect buzzing through the woodland air in the heat of summer. I replaced the bark and left it to its peace, but could not resist the urge to look for more. After two or three hours I had peeped into the chambers of another four or five and I returned home frozen-fingered but mightily pleased.

So, insects are alive and well in winter, even in the harshest of British Februaries, but they are hidden and dormant. The queen hornet's life is marvellously attuned to the seasons. In winter she sleeps but, for her species, this is a vitally important sleep. In her abdomen she carries the seed of the next generation and she must survive.

Spring will transform her life, releasing the instinct to forage and restore the energy reserves she will need to found a new colony. Summer will bring new queens and a generation of males to inseminate them. The old queen will probably die but not before she has had the opportunity to use all the senses and powers available to her. She has explored the world of vision, smell, touch and pain and has experienced, in her abbreviated life, all of the challenges that a year can bring. Insects are rarely granted the final challenge of growing old.

The hornet is only one of thousands of different species of insect whose lives are intertwined with the cycle of the seasons. This book attempts to chronicle some of the relationships, from the perspective of someone living in a temperate climate and for whom the usual connotation of the word 'seasons' is spring, summer, autumn and winter. Tropical and sub-tropical regions have their own seasons, but I have no experience of these and indeed some would argue that the countries of the Mediterranean basin, which come within the remit of this book, have really only two seasons: a wet (winter/spring) and a dry (summer/autumn). This arbitrary distinction is, I think, of less importance than trying to understand how insects cope with the challenge of their environment. If at times this means digressing into some of the more fascinating aspects of their physiology, I make no apology for it.

There must be readers who, like myself, find it a source of wonderment that any insect can survive the harshness of some of our winters. Just as intriguing are the effects that unusual or freakish climatic conditions may have on our local fauna. Even as I write, I have just experienced a case in point. Walking along a fenland footpath that I have known and frequented for nearly ten years, I heard a sound that instantly reminded me of Spain. It was the song of the great green bush

A well-disguised crab spider has succeeded in capturing a small bee.

cricket *Tettigonia viridissima*, an insect which is normally scarce away from the southern counties of England. Soon I had tracked it to its owner and within minutes perhaps half a dozen more had struck up. I have no doubt that the run of mild winters and exceptionally warm summers that has recently occurred in Britain has had a significant effect on the distribution of plant and animal life. As someone else commented in another context, if this is the greenhouse effect, give me more.

That first encounter with the queen hornet presented a challenge that I could not resist and over the intervening three years or so, I have endeavoured to put together a pictorial account of the subject as I see it. The project also gave me an opportunity to explore new ways of photographing insects in order to enhance the biological message that I wished to convey. Photographing a flying insect through the transparent wing of another, while maintaining perfect focus on both, is an intriguing problem. I had already acquired the methodology for taking pictures of insects in flight, but solving the simultaneity problem took a further year. Recording the moment of impact between a raindrop and a flying insect was almost as demanding, although thoroughly worth the effort involved, since it was only when I saw the images that I began to think seriously about the curious physical events that were occurring. Such images are designed to focus the mind but I must leave it to the reader to decide whether they have succeeded. In fact the greatest challenge lies ahead. If the reader, after perusing Chapter 3, becomes intrigued to know literally what the world looks like through the eye of a tiny insect, he or she will appreciate what fertile ground this presents for the invention of new kinds of photographic images.

1

SPRING: *A TIME FOR FEASTING*

WE ALL KNOW when spring is here because we can feel it in the air. We would be hard-pressed, however, to say exactly when it had arrived. The harder and closer you look for the telltale signs, the further you have to put back the clock. Traditionally the first reliable indicators are the spring bulbs which begin to brighten up the gardens: fritillaries, crocuses and daffodils. Snowdrops, winter aconites and hellebores appear earlier but, like the *Soldanella* snow-bells of the European Alps, they steal a march on what we would consider to be genuine springtime. The first splashes of floral colour in the countryside are a better guide since town gardens are generally warmer and better protected than the open fields and woodland.

In March or early April, or as early as February in the countries around the Mediterranean, the true harbingers of spring appear: coltsfoot, celandines, lilies and asphodels in exposed ground; the first orchids, cyclamens, white-flowered anemones and garlic in shadier woodland. Even in Britain and northern Europe, with their traditionally late seasons, one could go back as far as January and still find stirrings of springtime: the delicate shoots of dog's mercury and lords-and-ladies venturing up through the leaf litter on the woodland floor. Not very much later it is possible to find alder catkins and the diffident pink flowers of elm trees casting their pollen into the wind. In locations moist underfoot, mosses and liverworts have barely ceased activity throughout the whole of the winter, and the same can be said of the coral-like lichens clinging to old churchyard walls. So it is probably true to say that by the time most of us utter a sigh that spring is here at last it has, in fact, been around for months already: we just didn't notice the signs.

INSECT EMERGENCE

The same comments could be made about spring insects. The obvious indicators are the early butterflies that suddenly become noticeable hovering in the vicinity of flowers in the garden. These are mostly small tortoiseshell *Aglais urticae*, peacock *Inachis io* or brimstone *Gonepteryx rhamni* and the bedraggled appearance of many of them betrays the fact that they are last year's specimens that have just emerged from winter hibernation. Gradually lengthening daylight and steadily rising air temperatures are drawing out other hibernants such as queen bumble-bees and wasps. These are mated queens that have survived the winter hidden inside rotted tree stumps and are now seeking to fortify themselves on any nectar available, before commencing the business of founding the next colony of workers. Ladybirds such as the two-spot *Adalia bipunctata* and 22-spot *Thea 22-punctata*, illustrated in the photographs on page 189 (**214** and **215**), may be found massed together in hundreds or even thousands of individuals on sunlit vegetation prior to their post-hibernation dispersal, and following a series of warm days insects not normally seen throughout the year such as the stag beetle *Lucanus* and the lesser stag beetle *Dorcus* suddenly become noticeable in the hedgerows, appearing to synchronize their emergence from hibernation.

Mingling with these remnants of the previous year's generation of insects are individuals forming the vanguard of the new generation. These have spent the winter in larval form living in the soil, cocooned inside plant tissues or protected from the snow and frost inside rotten tree trunks and beneath deep leaf litter in woodland. Solitary bees such as *Nomada*, *Andrena* and *Halictus* become noticeable on spring blossoms such as blackthorn, apple, dandelion and, somewhat later, hawthorn. Flies appear on the scene, some of them, such as dung-flies, winter gnats and the occasional blowfly, having survived the winter as adults. Others, such as the St Mark's fly *Bibio* have just emerged from pupation in countless thousands and are already smothering the early cow-parsley flowers in their feverish search for nectar. Within hours of emergence, most of the females are already paired off with a male and inside their bodies nutrients are being channelled towards the developing ovaries in preparation for egg-laying. These are the fortunate ones that survive the depredations of another first generation fly, the carnivorous empid *Empis tessellata*, whose emergence seems timed to coincide with the explosive increase in numbers of its favourite prey.

All of these early insects are gripped by the same driving instinct, which is to feed. Insects are animals and, like all other animals, including ourselves, they have certain basic nutritional requirements. The ideal diet of an insect would not be very different from our own: it would be dominated by carbohydrate to provide the immediate energy needs of the body; it would contain suitable quantities of proteins needed for growth, repair and maintenance of tissues, and a modicum of fat to permit the synthesis of nerve and cell membranes and specific hormones; and it would be supplemented by traces of vitamins and minerals. Sodium, potassium and calcium are just as vital to the proper functioning of an insect's muscles and nervous system as they are for our own, although the lack of teeth and a bony skeleton lessens the need for a regular intake of large amounts of calcium.

THE SEARCH FOR NECTAR AND POLLEN

Of all foods, carbohydrate is the most plentiful and the most easily available, usually in the form of plant material. Insects have evolved every conceivable strategy for extracting food from plants and nowhere is this more apparent than in the diversity of their jaws: sturdy mandibles for chewing cellulose, including wood; stiff tubular beaks for piercing plant stems and sucking sap; or long, flexible probosces for probing the nectaries hidden in the deepest flowers. Nectar is almost the perfect carbohydrate since it is virtually pure sucrose, requires little further digestion in the gut and is absorbed for use by the body within minutes of consumption. Typically the sugar is present in a 30–40 per cent concentration, that is roughly 1 teaspoonful for every 2.5 teaspoonfuls of water. It is one of nature's free gifts and many insects are total addicts. They will even fight over it: witness butterflies jostling with wasps, hover-flies and blowflies on heavily scented ivy-blossom. Even insects that you would not normally associate with the benign practice of nectar-feeding cannot resist it, given the opportunity. Female mosquitoes, denizens of sultry tropical bedrooms, would as soon take a draught of nectar from a flower as a blood meal from a host, and the same goes for female horseflies. The carniverous empid fly shown enjoying a meal of flesh in the photograph on page 124 (**132**) might be seen a few minutes later using the same fearsome-looking rapier to hoe between the stamens and nectaries of a flower.

Of all nectar-seekers, bees are probably the most indefatigable and the extent to which they are specialized for their task almost defies belief. A bee's proboscis has an internal bore of about 1/40 mm and, in order to draw a syrupy solution of nectar along this capillary tube at the rate at which bees are known to sip, the bee needs to generate a negative pressure in its mouth of about 1 atmosphere. This is enough suction to cause a jerry-can to cave in. If the nectar were only a few per cent more concentrated, and therefore more sticky, the task would be almost impossible. But structural adaptation is only one part of the story. Bees and flowers have had millions of years to try to arrive at a perfect relationship and each is jealous of the other. The flower offers nectar as a reward for pollination and it uses colour as the principal advertisement for the nectar. Unfortunately many other insects in addition to the true pollinator are sensitive to colour and find the nectar irresistable. Some flowers are visited by perhaps a hundred or more different insects but of these only a few are of any real service to the flower. This is why many plants have evolved flowers that are craftily designed to keep out the thieves, including flies, beetles and bugs, whilst retaining access for the bees. A bee may have imprinted in its brain, or may acquire through experience, the keys to dozens of different flowers many of which need to be, literally, prised open by the bee and which then snap closed as soon as it has departed.

I came across a splendid example of this in my own garden, involving half a dozen different species of bee, only one of which had the necessary 'key' to securing both pollen and nectar. The flower was the leguminous *Senna*, commonly called bladder senna on account of the shape of its fruit (senna pods). The key-holder was the leaf-cutter bee *Megachile* shown in the photographs on pages 42 and 43 (**43** and **44**) prising open a flower by pushing upwards with its head against the upper petal or standard and pushing downwards with its hindlegs upon the wings and keel. Opening the throat of the flower in this manner requires considerable force because the keel is spring loaded, but once it is opened, not only is access gained to the nectaries but also, as the photographs show, the pollen basket on the underside of the abdomen becomes either dusted by the stamens or brushed by the hair-fringed stigma. The photographs on page 43 (**45** and **46**) show two of the robbers at work. Neither is able to open the flower properly to gain both nectar and pollen, but each has a different technique to gain either one or the other commodity.

Nectar is not the only source of simple sugars for insects, although it is probably the most concentrated. Even so, bees distil the solution further by repeatedly passing it between their honey-stomachs and their mouths until more and more fluid has evaporated and it has acquired the treacle-like consistency that we associate with fresh honeycombs. Plant sap also contains sugars but in very low concentrations: in order to obtain enough protein and other nutrients, aphids and scale insects take up large quantities of sap when they feed. The excess sugary liquid is excreted as honey-dew which, in its turn, provides food for attendant ants, who 'milk' the aphids for this delicacy. Sweet fruits are rich in sucrose and dextrose which are easily digested into glucose, and even alcohol produced by the natural fermentation of fruits provides sustenance for fruit-flies.

FIBRE AND PROTEIN

Nectar, sap and fruit juices are highly available forms of sugar but most of a plant's carbohydrate is locked up in the mainly unavailable form of cellulose. There is no doubt that the potential energy is there: after all, fossil fuels such as coal and petroleum are nothing other than modified cellulose. The problem is extracting the energy since only a few animals, insects or otherwise, possess the necessary enzymes enabling them to digest cellulose. Large herbivorous mammals such as horses, cattle, sheep and gazelles rely almost exclusively on cellulose for their energy requirements yet none of them can digest it unaided. The cellulose is broken down into simpler elements by micro-organisms resident within the alimentary canal. Micro-organisms not only release the simpler molecules, which can then be absorbed by the animal, they also use these simpler molecules to manufacture new proteins of their own. Therefore, by regularly digesting part of its bacterial flora, the animal gains protein into the bargain. The insect equivalents of herbivorous mammals are wood-eating termites and the larvae of beetles which feed on rotting wood or herbivorous dung. The larvae of longhorn beetles, which also develop in wood, are exceptional since they are able to manufacture their own cellulose-digesting enzyme.

Protein is needed to manufacture new tissue and it is not surprising that the protein demands of insects are greatest when they are young and growing. The carnivorous habit of young carabid and tiger beetles, lacewings, ant-lions and assassin bugs automatically guarantees a high protein diet. Adult bees subsist largely on a diet of nectar but provision the nests of their young with a mixture of honey and protein-rich pollen. The social wasps feed their young on chewed-up, regurgitated animal material, while the solitary wasps provision their cells with fresh, paralysed insects. The most spectacular of these are the spider-hunting wasps which tackle, and almost invariably vanquish, large tarantulas. Parasitic wasps, from large ichneumons to the tiniest chalcids and mymarids lay their eggs inside the bodies of larvae, or even inside the eggs of other insects: the developing grub is literally bathed within a supply of high-protein nutrients.

The protein requirements of adult female insects increase when they are about to lay their eggs and this often shows itself as a change in food selection. For example, when the ovaries of a house-fly begin to mature in preparation for egg-laying she develops a preference for a diet with a carbohydrate/protein ratio of about 7:1, as opposed to the normal ratio of 16:1. Female butterflies are confronted with a difficult problem since the nectar on which they feed is virtually devoid of protein, and mature ova can only develop at the expense of energy reserves laid down when the insect was a caterpillar. Tropical heliconiid butterflies are able to gain additional protein by sipping pollen grains as a suspension in nectar. Adult mayflies do not feed at all, nor do most stoneflies, and these insects are totally dependent on the energy held in store from their larval stages, both for their own subsistence, and the production of eggs.

1. Freshly emerged from winter hibernation, seven-spot ladybirds *Coccinella 7-punctata* seek nectar from early-flowering garlic mustard *Alliaria petiolata.*

1

2. Another winter hibernator, the ichneumon fly *Ichneumon suspiciosus*, investigates vanilla-scented blossom of *Mahonia aquifolium*. Flowering from mid-winter to early springtime, *Mahonia* is a rare source of nectar to insects breaking their winter fast.

2

3

3, 4. A field of spring buttercups grazed by horses bodes well for insects (**3**). The benefits to these first generation sawflies *Cephus* (**4**), which emerge from pupation in April/May and immediately begin to pair off, are obvious, since they feed directly on the pollen from the buttercups. Horse droppings support a whole community of larval and adult insects such as scarab beetles, rove beetles, dung-flies, borborid flies and sepsid flies whilst the horse itself yields reluctantly to the blood-sucking proclivities of the horseflies *Tabanus*, *Haematopota* and *Chrysops* and the forest-fly *Hippobosca equina*. Eggs of the bot-fly *Gasterophilus intestinalis* are laid on the horse's belly or legs, where they are attached to the hairs. The larvae probably gain access to the stomach through the mouth, as the animal rubs the site of irritation with its lips. Once there, the young maggots attach themselves to the lining. After development in the highly nutritious medium, they pupate and pass out in the animal's droppings.

4

5

5–7. Classic mythology has it that Prometheus stole fire from heaven in a giant fennel *Ferula communis* (**5**). Indeed this beautiful Mediterranean plant acts as a beacon to springtime insects. Umbelliferous plants like fennel and hogweed *Heracleum sphondylium* (**6**) produce thousands of tiny florets arranged into larger, much more showy units or umbels. Umbelliferous flowers are usually white or yellow in colour and produce nectar in copious quantities. The small size and simple structure of the florets make them accessible to a wide range of generalized pollinators such as wasps, flies, beetles and ants (**7**).

6

7 ▶

8

9

8–10. The proboscis of the lesser tortoiseshell butterfly *Aglais urticae* can probe the nectaries of deep-throated flowers like *Aubrieta* (**8**) but butterflies generally prefer flowers with shallow, tubular florets such as the dandelion *Taraxacum officinale* (**9**). When sipping nectar from a relatively shallow, bowl-shaped flower like *Allium*, a painted lady butterfly *Cynthia cardui* can effectively reduce the length of its proboscis, and enable its eyes to come closer to the flower, by bending the proboscis at its 'knee' (**10**). The knee joint gives the proboscis greater dexterity by allowing it to be manipulated from the base like an Anglepoise lamp.

10

11. A honey-bee *Apis mellifera* sips nectar from the base of the petals of a borage *Borago officinalis* flower whilst clinging to the coronet of stamens. Although the undersurface of the bee is making contact with the stamens of the flower this does not necessarily mean that any pollen will be transferred. Borage is one of a large group of flowers which are 'buzz-pollinated' by particular bees, including species of *Anthophora*, *Bombus* and the black carpenter bee *Xylocopa*, but not the honey-bee *Apis*. The anthers of buzz-pollinated flowers only release their pollen when stimulated by a high frequency sonic discharge from the appropriate bee. This jostles the pollen grains in the anthers, causing them to be shaken out like salt from a cellar. The pollination sound is audible at close quarters as a whine much higher in frequency than the normal buzzing of the bee's wings even though it is caused by the same wing muscles. Following the bee's practice, horticulturalists have now been able to increase the pollination of some economic plants, particularly those belonging to the potato family, by artificially buzzing their flowers with sound from a loudspeaker.

12. The solitary bee *Osmia* visiting *Geranium* flowers for nectar. Although *Geranium* is a shallow-throated flower, the central column of stamens still has to be negotiated by the bees before they can gain access to the nectaries lying between the bases of the petals. The bees handle this barrier with remarkable agility, using their purchase on the stamens to direct the proboscis quickly and accurately towards the nectary. Note how the entrance to the nectary is guarded by a double fringe of hairs which not only guides the proboscis but also prevents other, short-tongued insects from thieving from the nectaries.

12

13

13. The obverse side of the *Geranium* flower reveals the five nectaries each bearing a dab of sugary fluid consisting of about 30 per cent sucrose. Note the hair-fringed gap between adjoining petal bases through which the tongue must be protruded from the outer side of the petals. Although working 'blind' in this way, a practised individual of *Bombus pratorum* can process a *Geranium* flower within two or three seconds, including the 'access' time, i.e. the time spent landing on the flower and locating the nectary. *Osmia* takes much longer, although most of the extra 'dwell' time at the flower is spent sipping the nectar. The difference in dwell time is due to the differing lengths of the respective tongues of the insects: the longer tongue of *Bombus* presents a larger surface area to the tiny packet of nectar and it is therefore mopped up more rapidly.

14

15

14–16. Members of the flower family Malvaceae, which includes *Hibiscus*, cotton *Gossypium* and the mallows, produce large quantities of pollen which is eagerly sought after by bees. These two photographs show the bumble-bees *Bombus pratorum* (**14**) and *B. pascuorum* (**15**) feeding on the mallow *Lavatera. Lavatera* is an open, shallow flower and access is gained, as in *Geranium*, by grasping the central column of stamens. Each of the large pollen particles shown sticking to the hairs of *B. pratorum* is in fact an accretion of many smaller individual pollen grains. Photograph **14** shows a young flower with fully developed male anthers but no sign yet of the female styles which are embedded within the staminal column. In photograph **15**, pollen production has almost ceased and the female styles are beginning to protrude from the end of the staminal column. Photograph **16** shows an older flower in which the styles are now fully protruded, looking like a bunch of fibre-optic wires. They are probably being cross-pollinated by pollen grains brought by the bee from another, younger flower. In fact, photograph **16** is quite unusual since bees spend little time on older flowers, seeming to sense even before they land that nectar production has ceased.

16

◀ **17.** A bumble-bee *Bombus hortorum* collects nectar from florets of musk thistle *Carduus nutans.* Bumble-bees often spend a long time on a large thistle-head, systematically circling round and round, visiting each of the hundreds of florets in turn. By adroit use of its tongue a worker bee can work up to a hundred florets per minute.

18

18. A honey-bee receives a dusting of pollen on its head while probing for nectar from a caltrop flower *Fagonia cretica.* Most of this pollen will be transferred by elaborate combing movements of the legs to the pollen baskets of the hindlegs where, as seen in this photograph, they will be mixed with honey to form a dough. The only sites on a bee's body that are beyond the reach of the bee's grooming movements are the areas on the back and beneath the proboscis. Some flowers make use of this fact in order to maximize pollination by the bee by ensuring that their stigmas are positioned to make contact with precisely these 'safe' sites.

19

19–21. Procession of blossoms: from very early spring through to the start of summer British hedgerows are lit up by a series of blossoms, each with its own flowering period. The first pioneer to add colour to the winter scene is blackthorn *Prunus spinosa* which is avidly sought after by first generation solitary bees as well as by insects emerging from winter hibernation, such as the queen hornet *Vespa crabro* here seen tumbling in a shower of blackthorn petals (**19**). Blackthorn can appear as early as the beginning of March or as late as April or May depending on the severity of the winter. Next in the procession comes bird cherry *Prunus avium* and crab-apple *Malus sylvestris*, although these are localized and insufficient in numbers to feature regularly in the diet of

20

21

springtime insects. Hawthorn or may *Crataegus monogyna* (**20**) appears in May or June and is probably the most important of the common hedgerow blossoms for insects. Around the Mediterranean its beauty, vanilla scent and appeal to insects are all matched by the related medlar *Crataegus azarolus* (**21**). Of the widespread British blossoms, elder *Sambucus nigra*, honeysuckle *Lonicera periclymenum*, wild rose *Rosa canina* and bramble *Rubus fruticosus* appear next in line. Elder seems remarkably devoid of interest for insects, honeysuckle is visited by hawk-moths and long-tongued bumble-bees for its nectar, while rose and bramble are primarily pollen flowers.

22. The primrose *Primula farinosa*, is one of the earliest deep-throated flowers to appear in springtime. The narrow entrance to the corolla tube, blocked even further by the protruding pin-head of the stigma, is virtually inaccessible to insects except those with narrow thread-like tongues such as butterflies, moths and bees.

22

23 ▶

23–28. Cultivated spring bulbs (**23**, **24**) lack the distinctive scent of their wild relative the bluebell *Endymion non-scriptus* (**25**) but they provide a convenient source of pollen and nectar for insects emerging from hibernation when few other blossoms are available. Although the honey-bee *Apis mellifera*, here seen seeking nectar from a hyacinth (**26**), occasionally leaves the nest to forage on a fine winter's day, the bumble-bee *Bombus lucorum* (**27**) and the hornet *Vespa crabro* (**28**) only break hibernation when average daylength and air temperatures have risen above a certain threshold.

26

25

27

29

29–31. Some true flies or Diptera have unusually long probosces enabling them to probe even deep flowers that are normally visited by bees. The empid fly shown in photograph **29** normally uses its 'beak' for sucking the body juices of insect prey but it is just as practical for sipping nectar from flowers, in this case a mallow *Malva sylvestris*. Female mosquitoes regularly drink nectar as an alternative to blood, even though it may reduce their fertility owing to its lack of protein. Male mosquitoes feed exclusively on nectar. The bee-fly *Bombylius major* (**30**) not only mimics but also parasitizes solitary bees although its proboscis, unlike that of bees, cannot be retracted into the head. *Bombylius* has a restless disposition; even when feeding, it prefers to hover rather than land, maintaining contact with the surface of the flower through a delicate toe-hold (**31**).

30

31 ▶

32

33

32–35. If the cap fits, wear it: the 'skullcap' of the flower of the white dead-nettle *Lamium album* could almost have been tailor-made for one of its most frequent pollinators, the brown bee *Bombus pascuorum* (**32**). The cap even provides shelter from the rain. The anthers of the white dead-nettle flower lie just inside the cap, where their pollen can be conveniently browsed by, amongst others, the hoverfly *Rhingia* (**33**), although its articulated proboscis is too short to reach the nectaries at the base of the corolla tube. In this way the bee and the fly avoid competing for the same resources in the flower and, since the bee comes into much fuller contact with both stigma and stamens, it pollinates the flower. Similar relationships between the structure of the flower and the form and feeding habits of insects that visit it can be seen in other members of the mint family (Labiatae). Here (**34**) a hoverfly is content to stand on the lower lip of a ground-ivy *Glechoma hederacea* flower, dabbing the anthers with its proboscis. In the very similar flower of the red dead-nettle *Lamium purpureum* (**35**) a brown bee *Bombus pascuorum* searches deep into the corolla tube for nectar and in the process pollen is dusted on to the top of its head.

34

35

36. A typical sight around the Mediterranean in springtime: a hillside ablaze with flowers of the broom *Calicotome*. Brooms, like other members of the pea family Leguminosae, are highly specialized for pollination by bees.

37–39. The entrance to leguminous flowers is sealed by a spring loading mechanism and only bees have the required strength and intelligence to trip it. Photographs **37** and **38** show the floral mechanism of the meadow vetchling *Lathyrus pratensis* being tripped by the bumble-bee *Bombus pascuorum*. In photograph **37** the bee has just landed and, with antennae lowered, is thrusting its head against the upper petal or standard and beginning to push down on the keel and the two wing petals with its middle and hindlegs. In photograph **38** the wing petals have been forced down and the valvular swellings on their surfaces, which normally close off the throat of the flower like a pair of tonsils, have been withdrawn. The bee can now insert its head and proboscis deep into the throat and simultaneously, as the photograph shows, make contact with style and stamens on the underside of the head. Once the nectar has been sipped, the removal of the bee's weight from the platform allows the keel to snap closed and simultaneously the style and stamens are withdrawn. Photograph **39** shows the small skipper *Thymelicus flavus* stealing nectar from *Lathyrus pratensis* by simply hanging on to the platform of the flower and snaking its proboscis into the tiny 'butterfly hole' which still remains in the throat of the flower even when it is fully closed. Since the skipper's weight cannot trip the flower, the reproductive structures stay held tight within the keel and any risk of accidental pollination is avoided.

37

38

39

40. The common vetch *Vicia sativa* displays an open bowl of nectar on the tiny black stipule located at the base of each flower-stem. These extrafloral nectaries appear to be for the benefit of the ant *Lasius niger* which patrols up and down the flower-stems taking a sip from each nectary in turn. The plant also benefits because the ant is less likely to be tempted inside the flower, raiding the nectar and spoiling the pitch for the *bona fide* pollinators, bees. But the ant also bestows a direct service by jealously guarding the extrafloral nectaries and driving away other potential nectar thieves.

40

41

41, 42. Pendulous flowers such as the honeywort *Cerinthe* (**41**) and *Fuchsia* (**42**) are not only protected against the rain, but also against pollen and nectar thieves. Bees can readily cling upside down to gain access to the corolla tube. The tongue of the honey-bee visiting the honeywort flower is not long enough to reach the nectaries at the base of the flower, and it is probably collecting pollen from the stamens lying just inside the mouth; this conclusion is supported by the presence of full pollen baskets on the hindlegs.

42 ▶

43

43–46. Some pea flowers discriminate even between different species of bee. Flowers of the bladder senna *Colutea arborescens* are visited by a number of different species, but the true pollinator appears to be the leaf-cutter *Megachile*. Photograph **43** shows a side-view of *Megachile* on a flower that has just been tripped. The 'brow' of the insect is thrust against the standard, the fore and middle legs are resting on the wings and the hindlegs are pushing down on the keel. The style of the flower, which is itself tensed upwards, is poking out of the opened keel and making contact with the fox-coloured pollen basket on the underside of the leaf-cutter's abdomen. The style has a brush of hairs which evidently picks up pollen from the flower's own stamens and presents them to the pollinator. In this case the visiting insect's pollen basket is empty but in photograph **44**, where the visitor is viewed directly from behind, the pollen basket is filled with differently coloured pollen from at least two species of plant. Flower constancy, or loyalty to a single species of flower, is the exception rather than the rule amongst bees and insects generally. Also, note how *Megachile* makes clever use of the spurs on the inner side of each hindleg to exert downward pressure on the column of the style, and the ridge of the keel.

Photograph **45** shows an instance of nectar thievery by the bumblebee *Bombus pascuorum* which is unable to trip the flower but simply hangs on to the side of the keel and inserts its proboscis into the narrow slit between the standard and wing petals. *Bombus lucorum* makes a similar approach, but the honey-bee *Apis mellifera*, which is also unable to trip the flower, gains access to pollen in the keels of older flowers which have lost their spring loading and remain permanently tripped (**46**).

44

45

46

47

48

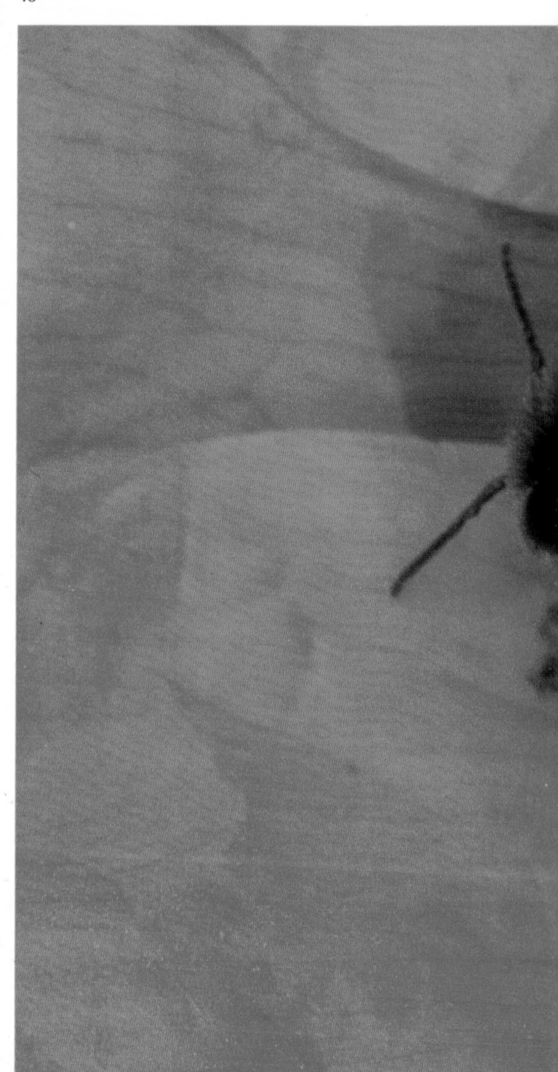

49 ▼

47–51. The cloud of pollen coming from these catkins of the alder *Alnus glutinosa* (**47**) contains tens of thousands of individual grains, each measuring only 1/50 mm or so in diameter. Although pollen is said to float in the air, it has a free fall velocity of about 2–3 cm per second. On a calm day this still allows 10 or 15 minutes before the pollen from a tall tree reaches the ground. Pollen is rich in protein, indeed this is one of the reasons why hay-fever sufferers react so badly towards it. It is also the reason why so many insects gather it. Some flowers such as rock-rose, bramble and poppy (**48**) are visited by insects specifically for pollen collection. Most of these pollen flowers have numerous stamens and visiting bees simply scrabble about in them covering their bodies in pollen as they do so. The pollen baskets of the honey-bee in photograph **49** are full of black poppy pollen. Pollen grains from the common mallow *Malva sylvestris* clump together to form larger granules which are visible to the naked eye. The honey-bee shown in photograph **50** is covered with these granules, drawn to its body by electrostatic charge, but the insect has not yet made any attempt to gather them together into the pollen baskets on its hindlegs. The bumble-bee in photograph **51** is also covered in pollen from a recently opened spear-thistle *Cirsium vulgare*. Notice the ripe anthers poking through the tops of the tiny tubular florets. Even the small capsid bug in front of the bee seems to be interested in them.

50

51

52

52. Oak is one of the last of the deciduous trees to sprout new leaves in springtime, but even before bud-break the eggs of oak processionary *Thaumetopoea processionea*, oak beauty *Boarmia roboraria* and green oak tortrix *Tortrix viridana*, moths are waiting. Compared with nectar and seeds, leaves are a very poor source of energy and consist mainly of fibre and water. To obtain sufficient energy and protein for growth, leaf- and grass-eating insect larvae need to consume many times their own weight in food. On the credit side, the food is immediately available, in almost unlimited supply.

53. Ants are like harvest mice on a smaller scale: they recognize the value of seeds as a concentrated energy source. The energy is usually in the form of starch, as in grass seeds (cereals), peas and beans, or oil, as in oilseed rape, sunflower seeds and peanuts. Another great advantage of seeds as a food source, compared for instance to nectar, is that they contain relatively little water and store well in a dehydrated state. Stability is a necessary requirement for the staple food of insects living in large societies. Unlike most insects, whose aim is to consume the food as soon as it is available, ants have first to forage for the food, deliver it to a central depot, and then mete it out over long periods of time to several generations of offspring which may be at different stages of development and may have different nutritional requirements. It is only provident behaviour like this that has enabled ants to colonize arid environments like deserts and dry grassland. The photograph shows *Messor* ants harvesting fresh seed from a flower-head of a crown daisy *Chrysanthemum coronarium*.

53 ▶

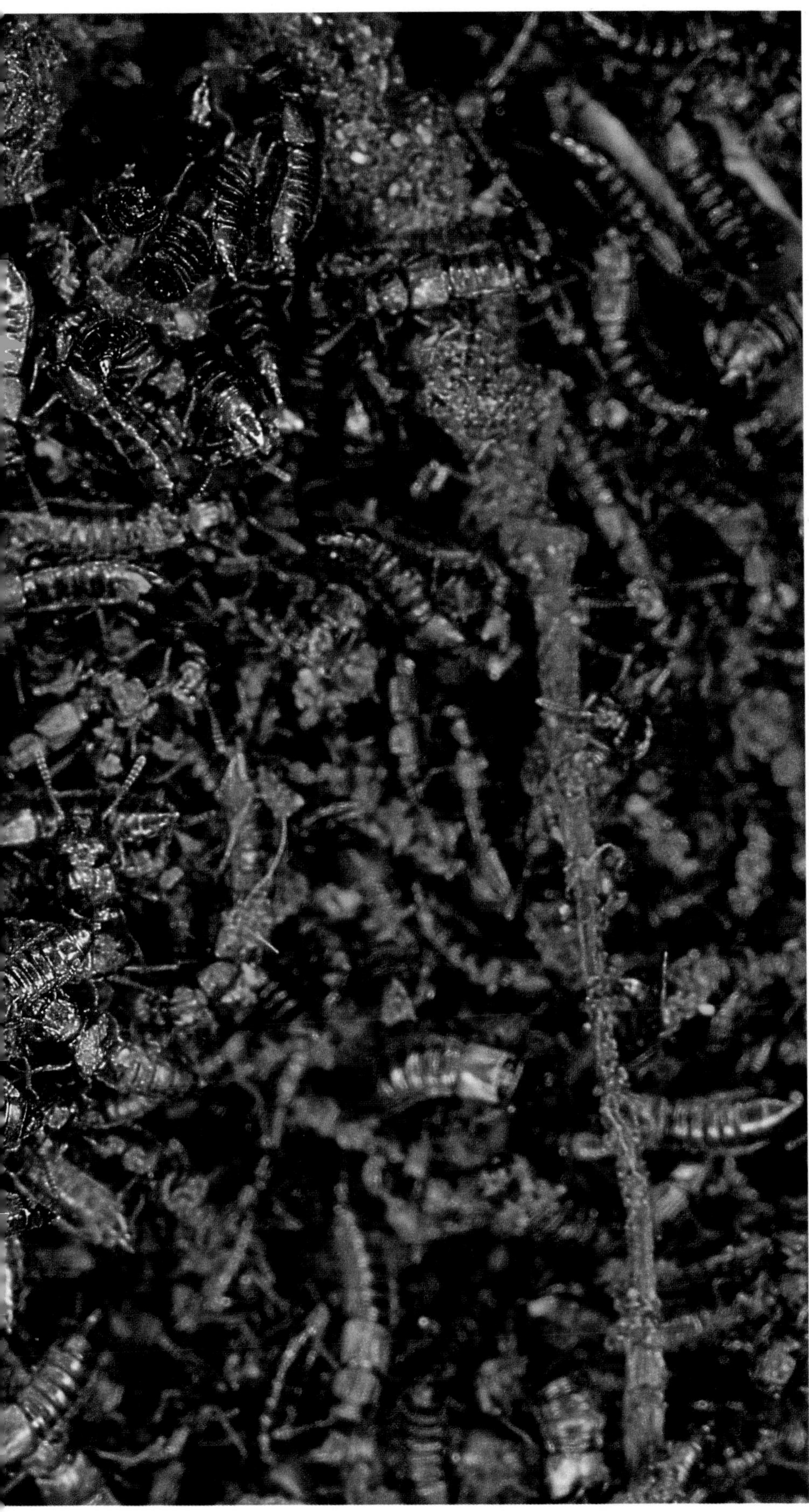

54

54. Scavenging is an effective form of feeding since it provides a wide diet of dead animal and plant matter, and animal droppings, most of which are relatively rich in nutrients. The rove beetles shown in this photograph are scavenging communally on dung, taking advantage of the fact that nutrient absorption by the mammalian bowel is often inefficient and leaves much unrecovered energy in the droppings. Most of this energy is in the form of partially digested fibre but there may also be a little protein in the bacterial flora evacuated from the bowel along with the droppings. Dung insects such as the scarab beetles *Geotrupes* and *Scarabaeus* spend most of their larval and adult lives in dung whilst others like the dung-fly *Scatophaga* and various species of rove beetle, develop inside the dung but as adults prey upon other insects in and around the dung. Amongst the more unlikely beneficiaries from dung are butterflies. It is not unusual, particularly in sunny weather immediately following rain, to see butterflies feeding from the surface water that has collected on the dung. They are using the dung as a kind of 'salt-lick' to obtain much-needed minerals and other trace elements that are virtually absent from their usual diet of nectar.

55, 56. The most efficient form of feeding, in terms of nutritional gain per unit of food consumed, is unquestionably carnivory. Not only is animal tissue richer in energy, protein and salts than plant material, but this energy is also much more easily extracted by digestion. Here a great green bush-cricket *Tettigonia viridissima* (**55**) is disposing of one of its smaller cousins, a conehead *Ruspolia*. Note how the barbed front legs are used to immobilize the prey. Chitin is a very hard material and predators like *Tettigonia* must be able to chew through it in order to get to the softer, more nutritious tissues. Zinc obtained from the diet is used to toughen the mandibles and their scissor-like movement has a self-sharpening effect on the edges.

A praying mantis (**56**) has only weak powers of flight and a set of jaws which are smaller than those of many of its victims, including the locust shown here. It relies on stealth, extremely accurate visual targeting and a lightning strike to trap its prey.

55

56 ▶

2

COURTSHIP AND REPRODUCTION

Exactly what it is that brings comfort and succour to an insect's life is a secret best left to the insect, but, from the point of view of an outsider, there would seem to be little question that to be warm, well-fed and in possession of a mate must feature high on the list of priorities. Of these three, the advent of spring provides the warmth, and for the others the insect must look out for itself.

For the female, feeding and reproduction often go hand in hand and in the previous chapter we saw how her diet becomes directed towards the growth and maturation of the eggs inside her ovaries. Mayflies and stoneflies, which do not feed as adults, and the majority of butterflies and moths whose adult diet is virtually pure sugar, have already developed their ovaries while in the larval or pupal stage. However, most insects once they are adult need a period of maturation before the eggs are ready to descend into the oviduct (ovulation) to await fertilization by the male sperm and eventual oviposition. During this period, which may last for only a few days, the eggs are becoming steadily filled with yolk consisting of protein, lipids and in some cases the high-energy carbohydrate glycogen. Naturally the female needs to be adequately nourished for the eggs to ripen properly in this way and mosquitoes and bedbugs ensure this by deferring ovulation until after a blood meal has been taken.

The female stable-fly *Stomoxys* can survive for weeks on a diet of nectar but her fertility suffers unless she is given access to blood.

FINDING A MATE

Finding a mate does not seem to pose a difficulty for the average female insect, at least to judge from the commonness of sights such as those shown in the photographs on pages 67 and 68 (**69** and **70**), where multiple male molestation is the main problem. Certainly the chances of encounter between male and female sawflies *Cephus* shown in the photograph on page 15 (**4**) are enormously increased because countless millions of individuals of the new generation all tend to emerge within a few days of one another in the spring. In other species, an innate swarming behaviour is designed to secure the same effect, although the swarming instinct is not always linked to mating. The proverbial swarming of locusts, and the massing together of thousands of post-hibernating ladybirds in early spring are a prelude to migration and dispersal. The most familiar mating swarms are the nuptial flights of ants, involving the appearance of a brief generation of winged males and queens. Swarming also seems to be related to a kind of fixation behaviour. The male ants just referred to will often cluster together in large numbers around a particular spot, such as a twig or stone before taking to flight. Swarms of the midge *Culicoides*, one of the true biting midges, select a particular cowpat above which to perform their endless side-to-side gyrations, whilst the St Mark's fly *Bibio* prefers to hover up and down into a slight breeze coming over a hedge-top.

Swarms are very dependent on weather conditions, as I can testify from watching the behaviour of a nest of black ants *Lasius niger* which had taken up residence in the wall of my house. Emergence of winged males and queens commenced in late July and for several days in succession the same pattern of behaviour would be repeated. At three or four o'clock in the afternoon workers would begin to appear at a number of pea-sized holes that had been excavated into the mortar. These groups of workers seemed to be 'testing the air', as it were and, once they were satisfied that conditions were right, they would then let out the males and queens who up until that point had been impatiently pressing at the door. Since the wall of the house was enclosed by a conservatory roof, the columns of ants would automatically begin working their way upward towards the light. If, during the course of this exodus, the weather began to change, for instance with the imminent approach of a rain shower, the whole operation was put into reverse and the workers started shepherding their charges back towards the nest. For their part the males and queens seemed like so many lost sheep, huddling together into small groups meekly waiting for their escorts. In fact, the workers were anything but gentle: hesitant queens or males would simply be hauled along by the antennae. Retrieving the stragglers might take two or three hours, but even by nightfall the doors to the nest would still be not quite closed and workers remained out on the walls, vainly trying to cut free individuals that had become snared in cobwebs in the more inaccessible corners of the conservatory.

During the course of long field excursions, I have become used to all kinds of insects swarming in the air just above the roof of my Land-Rover. These have included columns of male mosquitoes, characteristically whining; a small species of termite, which kept me awake at night by raining down on to the roof of the car; and mayflies, silent and altogether more graceful in their motion. These swarms usually occur at dusk and are often poised just above the rear edge of the roof. For a while I was mystified by their fastidious preference for this particular point until it dawned upon me that before nightfall I automatically park the vehicle with its nose pointing into the wind. Evidently this not only serves my own purposes by giving me more comfortable access to the rear of the car, but also those of the swarming insects, for whom the rear edge of the roof provides a convenient fixed line for holding station into the breeze.

Watching the hovering mayflies proved particularly instructive. First of all it was difficult not to feel that these little creatures were enjoying what they were doing. But secondly, and somewhat more seriously, it gave me an insight into the probable function of the three bristles that are seen to arise so conspicuously from the end of the tail of these insects. Each insect hovered up and down relentlessly through a vertical distance of several metres. During the upward movement of each cycle, the wings were beaten furiously in order to gain height quickly, and the three tail bristles were spread flat in their normal horizontal position. Once it had reached the summit of its path, the insect stopped its wings, held them in a stationary V-shape above the body, and then plummeted straight down. During the descent the body succeeded in remaining perfectly horizontal, the tail bristles now being bent upwards from the base like vertical streamers. From these observations, one had the clear impression that the bristles were being used to stabilize the body during the free-fall phase of its flight.

The great benefit of swarming is as a means of advertising to potential mates. The swarm is highly visible, not just because of the concentration of individuals, but because they are moving up and down or from side to side in a regular manner. As we shall see in the next chapter, the insect eye, though poor on form discrimination, is very sensitive to motion detection. Even so, such vision can only be effective over short distances, let us say a few metres. Moreover, sexual recognition by eye is often highly unspecific, with sometimes amusing results. For example, butterflies have been known to hurl themselves at anything that flutters, such as a leaf in the wind, and male ladybirds frequently assault other males or attempt to copulate with tiny ladybird-shaped pebbles. To attract mates from farther afield may require the use of chemical attractants, or aphrodisiacs, such as the pheromones secreted by the abdominal scent glands of butterflies and moths. These are known to be capable of exciting males from several kilometres downwind and, unlike vision, they are highly specific.

SINGING

Singing serves the same purpose of advertising over distance, up to a quarter of a kilometre in the case of the mole cricket *Gryllotalpa*. However, the head-tapping of the death-watch beetle *Xestobium*, as it sits inside its burrow in the wood, is audible only locally to other interested parties. Some unusual methods of sound production have come to light in insects, such as the hissing of the lepidopteran *Acherontia*, which sucks air in through the proboscis. The familiar buzzing of cicadas is produced by the high-frequency buckling of a drum-like membrane driven by a muscle attached to its inner surface. Most insect sounds, however, involve stridulation during which one part of the body, which is roughened into a file, is rubbed against another which acts as a scraper or plectrum. Grasshoppers are the most familiar example. In this case a row of pegs on the hind femur is rubbed against a ridge on the wing, and the pegs 'ping' in succession as they are struck by the ridge. Those readers who visit, or even live around the Mediterranean will be familiar with the incessant 'bleeping' sound made by the black field-cricket *Gryllus campestris*, one of the first of the evening crickets to strike up in succession to the day-time cicadas. This sound results from the rapid opening and closing of the truncated wings which causes the scraper of one wing to be drawn across the file of the other. Cricket sounds are almost pure tones and any shrill, piercing sound heard in the Mediterranean darkness is likely to be (if it is an insect!) the song of one or other species of these musically inventive creatures. Not all of these songs are strictly tied to mating. Amongst grasshoppers and bush-crickets different sounds may be produced as part of courtship, copulation, alarm or aggression and all are fashioned with different rhythms, tones and cadences.

Incidentally, there is one particular insect sound that has nothing to do with reproduction, and you might hear it if you place your ear close to an English rose. Bumble-bees visiting roses whine in a very excited manner as they scrabble about in the forest of stamens surrounding the centre of the flower. The whine is clearly audible but pitched well above the normal buzzing of the wings. Look very closely and you will see that as the whine is made the wings perform a scissor-like motion over the back. The amplitude of this side-to-side motion is only one or two millimetres and you would hardly know the wings were moving. The motion is remarkably reminiscent of the rubbing of the wings in *Gryllus* and the mechanism probably involves the main veins being made to 'ping' against one another. And the purpose of this sound in the bumble-bee? Probably buzz-pollination, a subject dealt with in the previous chapter.

MATING AND EGG FERTILIZATION

Once a female has been located by smell, sound or sight, she may turn out to be coy despite all the male's efforts and she will therefore need to be wooed. This is not just because she is being 'fussy'; courtship ritual is a way of ensuring that the suitor belongs to the right species and the right sex. Paradoxically, some of the most complex rituals seem to have been evolved by the least charismatic insects. The humble fruit-fly *Drosophila* is already well known to thousands of geneticists, but its amorous techniques deserve it a wider audience. A coy female fruit-fly will only make up her mind once she and her prospective mate have gone through a curious preliminary dance. It begins with him approaching her and drumming on her head with his front feet. This then releases the next stage of the dance where they shuffle from side to side facing one another. Finally, the male feels confident enough to spread out his wings and twist their leading edge downwards, a simple flourish that seems to be full of meaning to her because she now permits him to mount her.

A pair of empid flies that are involved in a similar courtship dance to that of the fruit-fly are shown in the photographs on page 62 (**61** and **62**). The males of many species of empid present gifts to the female as a prelude to mating, although it is often interpreted by insect watchers as a gesture of appeasement on his part rather than ingratiation. The male *Empis* shown in the photograph on page 124 (**133**) has just given to his chosen mate a present of a meal in the form of a St Mark's fly. Perhaps he is aware that, as far as she is concerned, once he has inseminated her he is dispensible and she may as well eat him. That way he will contribute directly to the next generation of empid flies by forming part of the yolk of his own offspring. By thinking ahead and preoccupying her, he may escape to live another day, and eventually mingle his genes with those of a second mate.

Physical pairing between insects usually involves the male embracing the female followed by interlocking of the genitalia, but male springtails place a packet of sperm, or spermatophore, on the ground and the female transfers it to her genital pouch. The pairing positions adopted during copulation vary according to species. The female-above position is far less common than the male-above, but scorpion-flies meet side by side, craneflies end to end and some hoverflies, such as those in the photograph on page 67 (**68**), end to end but with the male upside-down. More gymnastic postures can be seen in mating damselflies and the otherwise rather undemonstrative alder fly shown in the photographs on pages 65 and 64 (**66** and **65**) respectively.

Once the sperm has been transferred, it can remain viable in the genital tract of the female for months or even years, receiving nourishment from the secretions of her accessory glands. Sperm longevity is particularly essential in queen bees and wasps because they are inseminated in the autumn but are only ready to produce eggs that are ripe for fertilization after winter hibernation. Social ants, bees, wasps and termites carefully foster their young after they have hatched, and solitary bees and wasps provision the nest or cell in which the egg has been laid with food. Even earwigs jealously guard their eggs over winter and then shepherd their brood in springtime. In most cases, however, parenthood extends no further than carefully choosing the host plant or animal on which, or at least nearby to which, the eggs will be laid, usually cemented down in neat array. Locating a suitable host may not always be easy. The lovely ichneumon fly *Rhyssa*, whose wisp-like body may be seen hovering in the vicinity of felled pines in late spring and early summer, has to insert her ovipositor 'blind' through wood in order to implant her eggs into the grub of the giant wood-wasp *Sirex*. Queen cuckoo bees may spend hours hovering low over the ground searching for the entrances to the nests of bumble-bees in which they will deposit their eggs.

57

57. A noctuid moth, using pressure from its internal body fluids, everts its abdominal scent brushes. The aphrodisiac exuded by the associated scent glands is capable of exciting a male from a distance of several kilometres.

58

58. The elaborately plumed antennae found in the males of some moths and flies like this phantom midge *Chaoborus crystallinus* carry innumerable scent receptors capable of detecting female aphrodisiacs or pheromones.

59

60

59, 60. Winged queens and males of the black garden ant *Lasius niger* congregate at a conservatory window before beginning their nuptial flight (**59**). For a brief time the queen displays her prowess as a flyer (**60**) but after the nuptial flight she bites off her wings at the base.

61

62

61, 62. A pair of newly acquainted empid flies begin their mating dance (**61**). The male on the right, having located the female by a combination of sight and smell is now reinforcing the courtship bond by tapping her with his legs. In the process a further exchange of aphrodisiac may take place. When the pair finally couple (**62**) the genitalia of the male (left) have to be twisted through 180° in order to lock exactly into those of the female.

64. A male *Donacia* beetle prepares to mount the female. Most beetles copulate in the male-above position, usually grasping the edges of the female's wing cases.

64

63. Copulation in craneflies. The female is recognizable on the left by her more bulbous abdomen, swollen with ripe but as yet unfertilized eggs. The abdomen tapers to a stylus-like ovipositor, frequently mistaken for a sting. The male genitalia include a pair of claspers which grip the female genital valves but in order to do so the end of his abdomen must be twisted through 180°.

63 ▼

◀ **65.** Mating in the alder fly *Sialis* is a remarkably acrobatic affair with the male aligning himself directly behind his mate, grasping the end of her abdomen between his forelegs then arching his own abdomen forwards over his head to meet with hers. In the process, he swivels his thorax so that all four wings are brought to one side like a hand of playing cards.

66. Not even the contortions of mating alder flies can quite compare with the so-called copulation wheel assumed by mating damsel-flies, as diplayed in this pair of *Ishnura elegans*. During this engagement the male grips the female round the neck using the two pairs of claspers at the end of his abdomen, while the female arches her abdomen forwards and under in order to make contact with the sperm which is stored in accessory genitalia on the underside of the male's thorax.

67, 68. Two's company: the St Mark's fly *Bibio marci* (**67**) is one of the first of the new generation of insects to be seen on the wing in springtime, having spent the winter as a larva underground. Almost immediately after emergence the flies begin to pair off, wasting little time on elaborate courtship rituals. The flies mate in the tail-to-tail position but if alarmed will not hesitate to take off *in coitus*, both beating their wings furiously and endeavouring to fly in opposite directions. The bee-mimicking hoverfly *Volucella bombylans* (**68**) also mates in the tail-to-tail position but with the male upside-down.

67

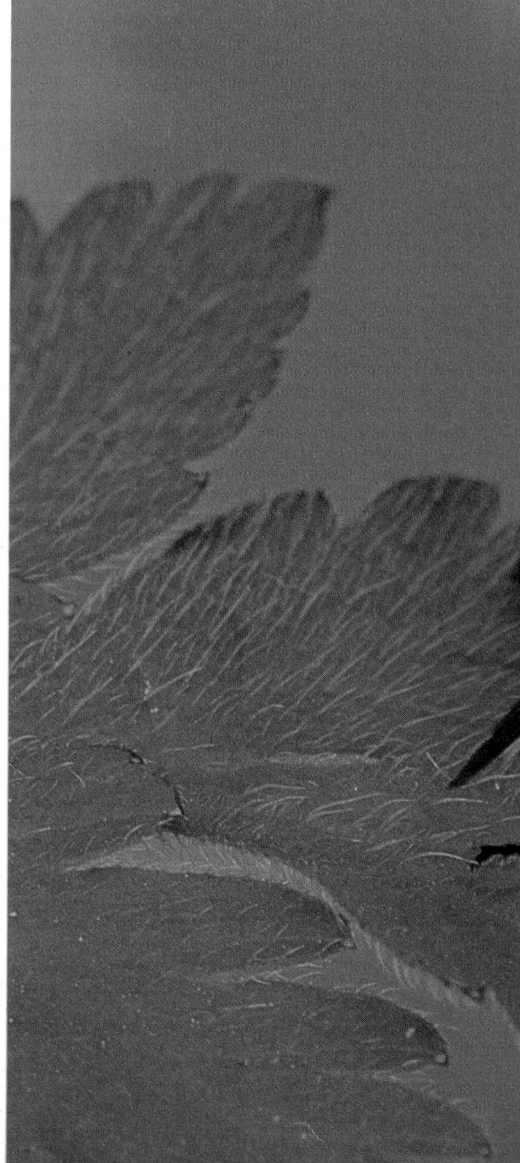

68

69. Three's a crowd. Unlike the St Mark's fly, the flesh-fly *Sarcophaga* mates in the male-above position. The third party in this case is a surplus male who may at any moment attempt to dislodge the active male and mate with the female himself.

69 ▼

70. Four? At the bottom of this curious 'kebab' of insect bodies lies a highly popular female sawfly *Cephus* in receipt of attention from three excited males. Only one however can possibly unite with her. Using her saw-like ovipositor, which gives this group of Hymenopterans its name, she will lay eggs in grass or cereal stems which will then be tunnelled by the larvae when they hatch.

70

71

71, 72. Wasps and bees are amongst the most assiduous of nest builders. In these two photographs a mason bee is seen constructing a nest of mud using its well-developed mandibles. Before egg-laying the nest will be provisioned with pollen and nectar providing food for the larvae until pupation.

72

73. The nest of the paper-wasp *Polistes gallicus* is made out of chewed wood mixed with saliva into a pulp. It contains a single layer of cells attached by a narrow stalk to rock, walls or vegetation. The grubs will be fed on insects caught by the adults but the nest will be abandoned once the breeding season is over. In contrast, impregnated queens of the related common wasp *Vespula vulgaris* sometimes use the old nest as an overwintering site.

73

74

75

76

74–76. The female alder fly *Sialis lutea* lays up to 500 eggs carefully arranged into a number of columns along a rush or grass stem (**74**). Although the alder fly larva is aquatic, it makes sense for the female to lay the eggs just above the water in order to protect them from predators below. Nevertheless, the eggs must be able to resist wetting in case of flooding and photograph **75** shows how an immersed egg mass becomes enveloped within a collar of air, visible as a glistening air/water interface. The tiny pits showing through the air collar, and giving it the appearance of a cheese grater, are the tiny projections on the outer ends of the eggs which are the only wettable parts. Rafts of mosquito eggs, looking like boats at harbour in photograph **76**, consist of hundreds of eggs wettable at only one pole, the one in contact with the surface of the water.

77, 78. Insect eggs are usually laid on, or close to, the host plant or animal upon which the larvae will develop. These eggs of the shield bug *Eysarcoris fabricii* (**77**) have been stuck down on to the underside of the leaves of the host plant *Stachys sylvatica*, the hedge woundwort, in order to provide protection from predators, the rain and excessive sunshine. During hatching, the egg splits open along, or in the vicinity of, a fracture line clearly visible in the eggs of the parent bug *Elasmucha grisei* shown in photograph **78**.

77 ▼

78 ▶

79

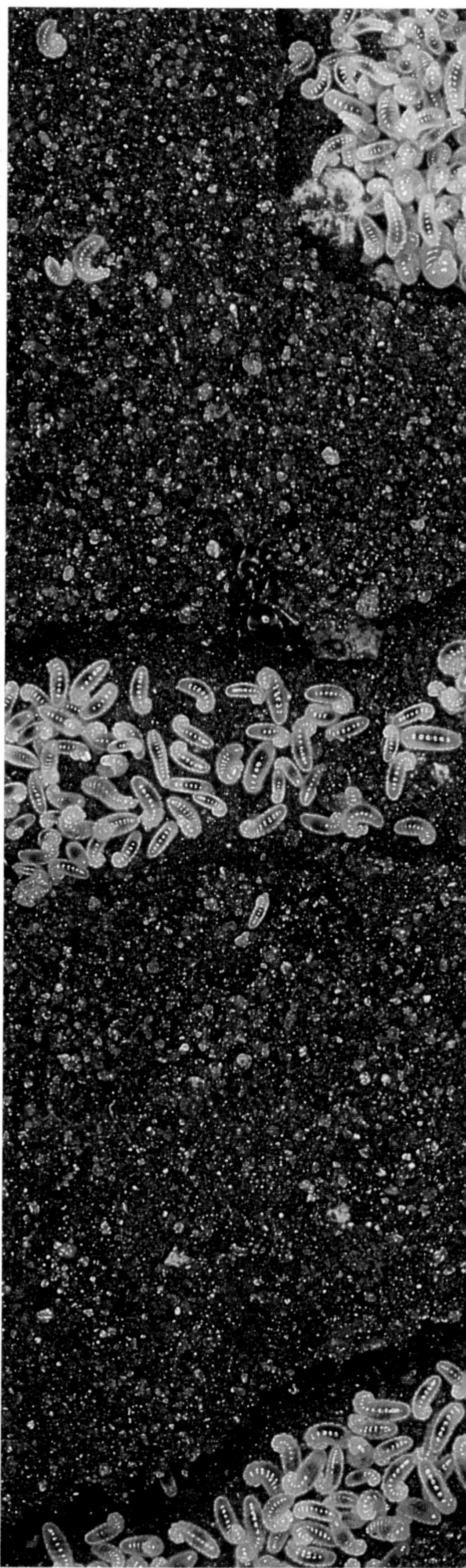

79–81. Apart from selecting an appropriate host plant or animal upon which to deposit their eggs, most insects make no further effort to ensure the survival of their offspring. The main exceptions are social wasps, bees, ants and termites although certain hemipteran bugs display what can be interpreted as altruistic behaviour. The parent bug *Elasmucha grisea* (**79**), for instance, stands guard over both eggs and young nymphs. The black garden ants *Lasius niger* shown in photograph **80** have carefully laid out their grubs in the upper galleries of their nest to receive maximum warmth from the sun. In photograph **81** a family of brightly coloured nymphs of a pentatomid bug are being shepherded by their parents into the safety provided by one of the various kinds of 'barbed wire' bush typical of the scrubby, sub-desert habitat in which they live.

80

81

82

82–85. Free-living caterpillars of moths and butterflies have various ways of protecting themselves from predators. Caterpillars of eggar, lasiocampid and tiger-moths are usually covered with hairs that release irritant chemicals when broken. Tiger-moth larvae live gregariously (**82**), cutting a swathe through the low vegetation upon which they feed and periodically resting to perform synchronized moultings on the spot. The benefits of living in such a colony are apparent because when an individual becomes separated from the rest (**83**) it fails to grow and develop at the normal rate. Communal living is even more developed in the larvae of processionary moths which inhabit 'tents' spun upon their host plant, usually a tree. This provides a refuge from which the larvae can make feeding forays on to the leaves, and into which they can retreat when under threat. The nest of the pine processionary moth *Thaumetopoeia* shown here (**84**) is structurally reinforced from inside by the steady accumulation of a debris of larval skins and droppings. The feltwork of silken fibres around the nest allows the larvae to bask on the surface, free of threat from enemies (**85**).

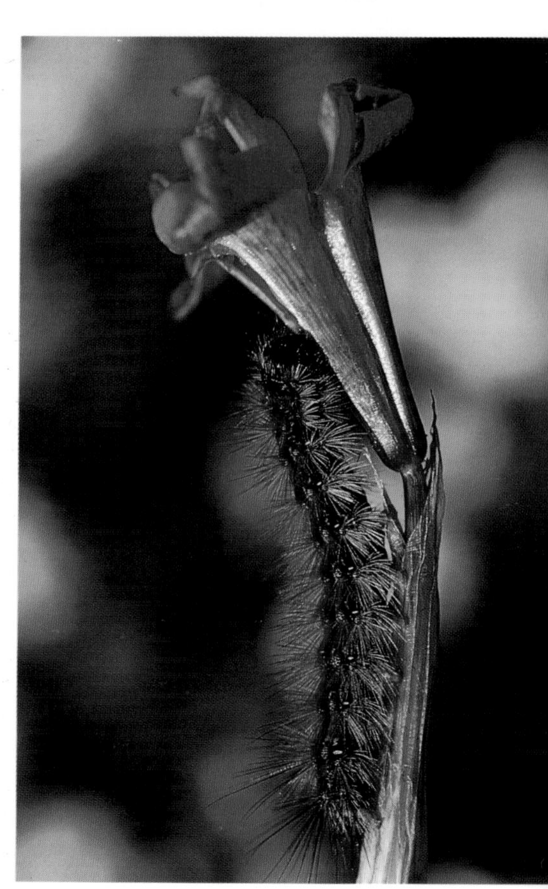

83

84

85 ▼

86. This sawfly larva is naked of protective hairs but is coloured a brilliant chalky white, advertising to potential enemies that it is obnoxious to the taste. Possibly it has derived digitalis-like chemicals from its host plant, the figwort *Scrophularia*, a relative of foxgloves.

86

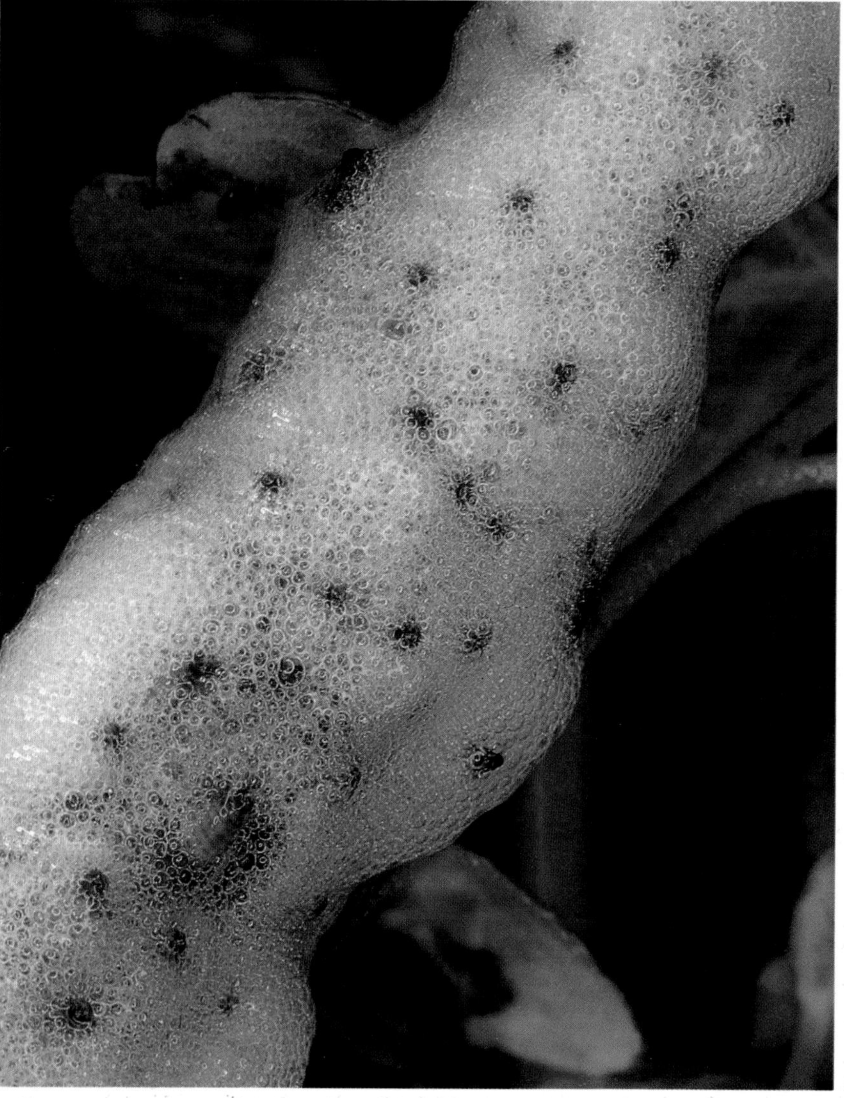

87

87, 88. The nymphs of froghoppers (Aphrophoridae) are protected inside frothy 'cuckoo-spit' (**87**). The tiny dots visible on the surface of the froth in the photograph are the ends of the abdomens of the nymphs, pushed through in order to breathe. This is the only non-wettable part of the body; if the nymphs are removed and placed in water, they hang from the surface like waterboatmen (**88**).

88 ▶

89, 90. The development of the wings of immature insects lags behind that of the rest of the body. The young of grasshoppers, crickets, mantids and true bugs are usually agile runners and jumpers and this compensates for the lack of flight ability. In these leaping nymphs of the mantids *Mantis religiosa* (**89**) and *Empusa pennata* (**90**) the rudimentary wings are just visible as two pairs of buds above the middle and hindlegs.

◀89

90

91, 92. Since insect cuticle can stretch to only a very limited extent, growth takes place through a series of quantum leaps or moults in which the old skin is separated from the new by digestive moulting fluid, then sloughed off in the process of ecdysis. The rather spectral object shown in photograph **91** is the cast skin of the grasshopper *Acrida*, and is virtually a complete replica of its former inmate, down to the claws at the ends of the feet. Photograph **92** shows a recently moulted larva of the mullein moth *Cucullia verbasci* hanging by its claspers from the old skin.

91

92

93

93–95. This nymph of the leaf-hopper *Cicadella viridis* (**93**) has recently undergone its final moult exposing the soft, curled-up wings. Aided by blood pressure, the wings will gradually expand to full size (**94**). If alarmed at this stage, a young adult will leap into the air but will not risk unfolding its delicate wings (**95**).

94

95

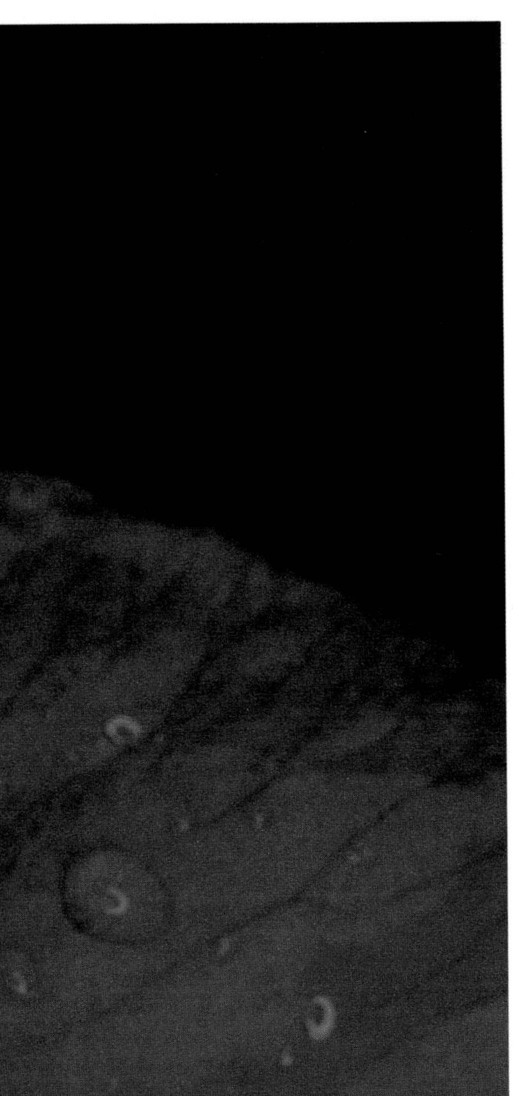

3

AN INSECT'S EYE VIEW OF THE WORLD

WITH SUMMER IN full swing and air temperatures climbing to their highest, the heat and the sunlight combine to drive insects to a pitch of activity. The days are long and offer little respite from the struggle to survive and the pursuit of the senses. One cannot fail to be impressed by the energy with which insects address themselves to an array of tasks that might daunt the average human being: defending territory, fending off rivals and predators, displaying, singing, hunting, digging, finding a suitable mate and of course the relentless search for food. Coping with the challenges posed by these activities calls for the deployment of the full range of primary senses with which insects are endowed: smell, taste, touch, hearing and vision. Some insects such as ants, termites and soil-dwelling larvae inhabit an essentially tactile and chemical world which it is difficult for most of us to imagine, living as we do in a world dominated by vision and images. But to what extent is it even possible to reconstruct the visual space of an insect, and how does it compare with that which we perceive through our own eyes?

INSECT VISION

Even if we knew nothing at all about the nature of the insect eye we might be tempted to guess at some of the tasks that it should be able to perform. For example, since insects are generally quite tiny animals which spend a lot of their time in very close contact with equally small or even smaller objects, should we expect them to have excellent close range vision including the ability to discern tiny details of size, two-dimensional pattern and three-dimensional shape? At the other extreme, since many of them fly in the air at considerable distances from any other objects, ought they to have good long-range vision as well, in order to see exactly where they are and where the best place is to make a landing? Take colour as another example: the bodies of some insects are covered with intricate, coloured patterns, but does this mean that the insect itself can actually see these patterns?

In fact, the answer to all three of these questions is 'no'. So, from the start, we see that preconceptions based on our own experience of the visual world are probably going to lead to error if we try to use them to interpret the insect's visual world. It is obvious that the insect thrives using the particular senses that it possesses, so the real challenge is to identify what qualities of the insect eye fit it to the demands of its *own* experience, not ours.

An eye is not just an optical system; it is an optical system plus a brain. We can study the optical performance of the eye but that will not tell us everything that the brain 'sees' behind the eye. Nevertheless it at least shows us the raw physical information that is received and upon which the brain can go to work, and fortunately we are readily furnished with the tools for assessing it. Visual acuity is one of these tests and this measures the ability of the eye to resolve detail. It constitutes the main part of a routine eye examination before an optician prescribes spectacles. The test object can be conveniently presented as a vertical grid of closely spaced, alternating black and white lines, although opticians generally prefer a more 'user-friendly' array of gradually diminishing letters of the alphabet. If the optician wants to speak to a scientist he can avoid ambiguity by defining visual acuity as the smallest angle that two closely spaced lines or dots subtend at the eye. The central field or fovea of the human eye can resolve about one sixtieth of a degree and the image in this area is composed of a mosaic of several hundred thousand 'pixels'. The visual field of both eyes combined is roughly 180° from side to side and 100° from top to bottom although the acuity in the peripheral field is very much inferior to that in the fovea. The foveal image is effectively 'grain-free' and in fact, purely at the level of optical performance, no camera lens can beat it.

As an instrument for resolving detail, the insect eye is abysmal by comparison. Curiously, the image that can be seen through the eye of a glow-worm was photographed many years ago and it would be far beyond the abilities of an optician to correct it. Quantitatively, the visual acuity of most insects is no better than 1 or 2 degrees. If an insect had the same visual field as a human being its 'image mosaic' would be composed of not several million, but only about twenty or thirty thousand points of light at best. This is not difficult to understand when you look at the structure of its eye. The photograph on page 95 (**100**) shows a close-up of the compound eye of a mantis and you can see that the surface is divided up into a network of facets. Each facet is a tiny lens which transmits light inwards along a cone-shaped element or light guide called an ommatidium. The whole eye consists of an array of such ommatidia all radiating inwards until they end on a feltwork of nerves deep inside the eye. This bundle of nerves is highly refractile and appears in some eyes as a black spot or 'pseudo-pupil' and it can be seen in the photograph. The pseudopupil appears to move over the surface of the eye as you look at it from different angles, giving the slightly eerie impression that the insect's eye is following you. In fact, this is an illusion because insect eyes are fixed.

The least grainy images are probably formed by the dragonfly compound eye shown in the photograph on page 93 (**98**). This has about 30,000 facets although less than a dozen facets may be present in the eyes of some insects living underground or in caves.

If insect eyes can render only a rather fuzzy reflection of the visual space around them we might also expect their perception of shape to be limited. Indeed it appears that bees do not recognize geometrical configurations such as circles, squares or ellipses but they are attracted to irregular shapes with broken contours. They display even greater interest if the shape is moving, like a flower swaying in the wind. Therefore, pattern itself is less important to insects than changes in shape and movement. They are startled by the rapid movement of sufficiently large objects across their field of view, irrespective of their shape.

Again, the science of human vision offers us an accurate tool for measuring the eye's sensitivity to moving images. A series of images presented to the eye in rapid succession, as in cinematography, fuses at a certain frequency. The frequency at which the flicker effect is lost is called the flicker fusion frequency and in man it is about 50 per second, the same as the mains electricity supply. Some insects however have a flicker fusion frequency of nearly 300 per second, so what appears to us as a 'movie' registers on their brain as a slide show. The rapid image-capture of the insect's eye equips it perfectly for apprehending movement and this is why shapes appear more interesting when they are moving. This has led to the conclusion that insects perceive shape and form, not as spatial geometries, but as varying degrees of flicker or, more technically, changes in visual 'flow'. Happily it is not beyond us to gain some impression of what this curious visual world of the insect must be like, but first we must remove our own veil of intellect. This is exactly what happens when suddenly from the corner of our eye we see a missile hurtling towards us. In an instant we will have reacted, not to the shape of the object, which will not have had time to register on the brain, but to its size and its velocity. By shutting out, even for a few moments, the image-based dominance that the cerebral cortex exerts over the rest of our brain, we catch a glimpse of the 'moving shadow' world of insect vision.

An insect's vision is tuned to its practical needs: it is less influenced by tangible qualities such as shape and pattern than by change: whether an image is getting brighter or darker, whether it is expanding or contracting. These simple cues will elicit, for example, an escape response to a shadow, a landing response to expansion (the ground is getting nearer) or a steering response to avoid or catch an object in flight. A notion of 'sufficient unto the day' is incorporated into the design of their visual system. For example, a water-strider spends its day skulling about on the surface of the pond keeping an eye out for predators, prey and other water-striders. All the meaningful things in its life happen along a narrow, horizontal line in space. Its eyes can perceive the full 360° of the pond surface around it, using only 920 pixels and 10 per cent of these are concentrated in a narrow row along the equator, the visual streak.

MEASURING DISTANCE

Even casual observation suggests that insects must be capable of making reasonably accurate estimates of distance, at least in the close range. A mantis will strike only when its prey comes within 2 or 3 cm of its head and likewise a tiger beetle, although it can see prey at a distance of 15 cm, waits until the prey is just in front of its mandibles before snapping. When male hoverflies chase one another they can hold a set distance between themselves accurate to within a centimetre. How does an insect measure distance? The methods available to it are more limited than those of birds and mammals. These animals, including ourselves, have eyes that can move in their sockets and can thereby be made to focus on the most sensitive area of the retina, the fovea, which receives light from the centre of the visual field. By slightly converging the eyes so that the foveal axes of both eyes intersect on the object, its distance can be computed. Another advantage of the human eye is that it can be accommodated, that is the curvature of the lens can be altered by muscle action, changing its focal length and allowing it to focus on a nearer or more distant object. Again, the brain can interpret the amount of accommodation that is required to achieve focus as a measure of the distance that the object is away from the eye.

Insects can neither move their eyes nor re-focus their ommatidial lenses. However, they can certainly move their heads. Anyone who has taken the time to watch a grasshopper preparing to leap from one spot to another will have noticed that it makes rather deliberate peering movements towards the intended point of landing. The whole body sways from side to side, like a compass needle, pivoted on the end of the abdomen. At the same time the grasshopper makes sure that its head and eyes are kept fixed firmly on the object. The pivoting movements of head on neck and body on ground make the whole process strangely reminiscent of an oriental dance. The serious purpose of the grasshopper, however, is to exploit the optical principle of motion parallax: by moving its head from side to side the image of the object will be made to move by a greater or lesser amount across the eye, depending on how far away it is. The grasshopper's brain performs the appropriate trigonometry, converts the computed distance directly into the required speed and trajectory needed to reach the target, and issues the command to jump.

Hoverflies in hot pursuit of rival males use another method of distance assessment which relies on the fact that as an object approaches the eye its image gets bigger, and progressively more and more ommatidia become stimulated by it. For this to work properly it helps to have a perfectly fixed gaze and a high concentration of ommatidia right in the centre of the visual field. This probably explains why in some male, but not female, hoverflies the gap between the front of the eyes is bridged by an extra band of ommatidia. It also explains why they orientate their bodies directly towards an object of interest whenever they change position, since, unlike grasshoppers, they cannot roll the head on the neck in order to maintain eye fixation. Male house-flies have a similar 'love-spot' or zone of acute vision on the inner corner of each eye, dedicated in their case to pursuit of the female.

Neither of the methods so far described depends on binocular vision: one eye will do. But it is known that one-eyed mantids, tiger beetles and dragonfly larvae rarely succeed in catching their prey. The same goes, incidentally, for raptorial birds. Predatory insects need to use stereoscopic vision for the extremely accurate targeting of their prey. Each of the compound eyes has a foveal region over which the constituent ommatidia collect light from a much smaller angle of the visual field. This means that this particular part of the visual field is served by an unusually high number of ommatidia compared with the peripheral field. The reason why a tiger beetle waits until prey is just in front of its head before seizing it is that the foveas lie on the inner side of the eyes and their axes intersect just in front of the jaws. When an object stimulates both foveas, the tiger beetle can be sure that it is at exactly the right range.

Mantids also have foveas, but they point directly forward and the foveal axes are therefore parallel. The foveas are still used as the reference lines for locating the prey but this time the mantis needs to compute the angle between the foveal axis and light rays coming from the object. In fact, it cocks its head slightly off-centre from the prey so that it is able to compare these angles in the two eyes. Mantids also use their peripheral vision to initiate quick head rotations in response to objects of potential interest appearing in the lateral field. These are similar to the jerky 'saccadic' movements made by the human eye while scanning. In both cases, the rapid movement serves to bring the object of interest directly into the field covered by the foveas where it can then be scrutinized more closely.

THE MEANING OF COLOUR

The sensation of colour is very subjective and any two human beings will disagree over the precise identification of hues. So trying to decipher an insect's appreciation of colour is something of a minefield. The first problem is that the insect's light spectrum is shifted downwards towards the shorter wavelengths compared with our own, so even if it did have a similar colour detection system to our own, its rainbow would not read red, orange, yellow, green, blue, violet. Instead, at least as far as bees are concerned, red is invisible but, at the other end of the scale, they can see ultraviolet.

Incidentally, we ourselves fail to see UV only because it is absorbed by the lens in the eye. People who have had the lens removed surgically see UV quite well. We know that insects can see UV because, amongst other things, moths will fly towards UV-transparent glass, which is opaque to our eyes, in preference to a bright blue window;

and, using UV, bees can orientate themselves with respect to the sun, even when it is completely covered by cloud.

It is said that bees have 'trichrome' vision because their compound eyes contain three visual pigments which absorb light most effectively at wavelengths corresponding to the colours yellow, blue and UV. However, these are only the peaks of the absorption spectra and there is a lot of overlap between yellow and blue, and blue and UV pigments. Each of the three pigments is located in a different photosensor and, by comparing the signals from any two photosensors, the brain is capable of discriminating the various hues. Thus, by having only three types of photoreceptor, the bee's brain is not limited to seeing only three colours. The principle is similar to that of a modern colour film which is coated with six different 'chromes' or emulsions but of course is capable of rendering every nuance of colour that the human eye can see.

The perception of colour is intricately tied up with brightness, and brightness itself is a highly subjective quality. Colours can only be seen in light of sufficient intensity; they cannot be distinguished in dull light or twilight. When presented with lights of different colours but equal intensities (real brightnesses), people see yellow as far brighter than the rest. A field of brilliantly glowing oilseed rape looks much brighter than the surrounding green corn but this is an illusion: both have the same objective luminosity. Interestingly, most insects suffer from the same illusion because the apparent luminosity of yellow is also greatest to them. This does not mean that they are all necessarily attracted to yellow above all other colours, no more than people prefer bright yellow clothing.

A bee's sensitivity to UV affects its vision in ways that we can hardly imagine. Although bees cannot see red, they do visit red flowers such as poppies, but they are attracted by the UV light reflected from them, not their redness. The light from a sunny sky must seem brilliant to a bee but at the other extreme the closing in of night after sunset will happen very quickly. An insomniac bee will be aware of a full moon simply as a diffuse blob of light in the sky, but will be unable to resolve its circular shape. It is unlikely that any nocturnal moth has ever been capable of seeing Sirius, the brightest star in the sky.

White as seen by bees is also different from the way we perceive it. White light is pure light because it is composed of all visible wavelengths equally mixed. Visible, that is, to us. But a white flower will look blue-green to a bee unless it also reflects UV. Red flowers will look black to a bee unless they simultaneously reflect UV. Butterflies, however, can see red, green and yellow, and this may affect their preferences for flowers.

96. A simple demonstration that some insects have an in-built response to light: in a darkened room, a group of leaf-hoppers crawls towards a burning candle. However, not all insects would show the same behaviour: some, such as those that habitually live in the dark beneath stones, under bark or in leaf litter, shun the light, as do shade-dwelling insects such as mantids and stick insects. Although moths are drawn magnetically to a brightly lit window at night, this is a highly artificial situation and the same moths, caught and released during the day-time, would immediately head for deep shade.

97, 98. The insect's visual world is unlikely to be the same as ours. This photograph (**97**) is approximately what the world would look like to an insect equipped with a scaled-down version of the human eye. The thing that a real insect would find most disconcerting about this world is its restricted field of view: with this human eye it can see in front, but not above, below, to the sides and behind. The real insect's brain would also be completely overwhelmed by the level of detail in the imagery. The fovea of the human eye (the most sensitive region of the retina) is served by more than 100,000 photosensors, and millions more cover the peripheral visual field. Now look at the compound eye of a dragonfly (**98**), one of the most sensitive of all insect eyes. Its field of view is almost global: the insect can see virtually in all directions using both eyes. But its resolution of detail is an optician's nightmare. The whole of this global field is mapped on to the dragonfly's brain by only 40,000 pixels – roughly the number of facets on the two eyes. The insect's brain is wired to deal with a highly granular image: any finer resolution would be superfluous.

98

99

99, 100. The butterfly in the foreground (**99**) sees its partner flying past in the background, but can it gauge how far away its partner is? One insect that measures depth and distance with precision, at least at close range, is the praying mantis (**100**). The mantis uses its binocular vision to estimate the distance of its prey before striking. It does this by comparing the angles at which the light rays coming from the object strike the left and right eyes. This method of angular disparity works best if the eyes are widely spaced on the head, a characteristic of both mantids and the predatory larvae of dragonflies. The black spots on the mantid's eyes look like pupils but this is an illusion. The 'pseudopupil' is an image of the core of the eye which is filled with the highly refractory nerve endings attached to the array of retinal elements radiating inwards from the facets on the surface of the eye. It is analogous to a large black pip in the centre of a transparent apple. The pseudopupil appears to move over the eye as you view it from different angles. Since in this case the mantis is viewing the observer askance, the pseudopupil appears on the inner corner of one compound eye and on the outer corner of the other.

100

101

101. How quickly can the insect eye capture the image of a rapidly moving object? This is obviously important during flight, with terrain moving rapidly past, or during hunting when trying to track the movements of prey. The image-capturing abilities of the visual system are assessed by measuring the flicker fusion frequency: the critical frequency at which a sequence of light pulses appears to fuse into a continuous source of light. In this particular department, many insects excel over human beings in performance. The frequency at which stroboscopic light becomes continuous to our eyes is roughly equivalent to that of mains electricity: 50 cycles per second. For the bee, the corresponding figure is 55 but a blowfly can resolve nearly 300 consecutive images per second: what would appear as a 'movie' to the human eye is seen as a slide show to the insect eye. So it is quite likely that the insect in the foreground of this photograph can freeze the flickering motion of the wings of the insect flying behind it.

102. Not for our eyes . . . springtime flowers in a Tunisian landscape. As long ago as 1793 the German scientist Sprengel recognized that flower colours were evolved for their pollinators and not for human aesthetic appreciation. The association between insects and flowers is arguably the longest marriage of all time. It reaches back hundreds of millions of years to the time when flowering plants first evolved on the

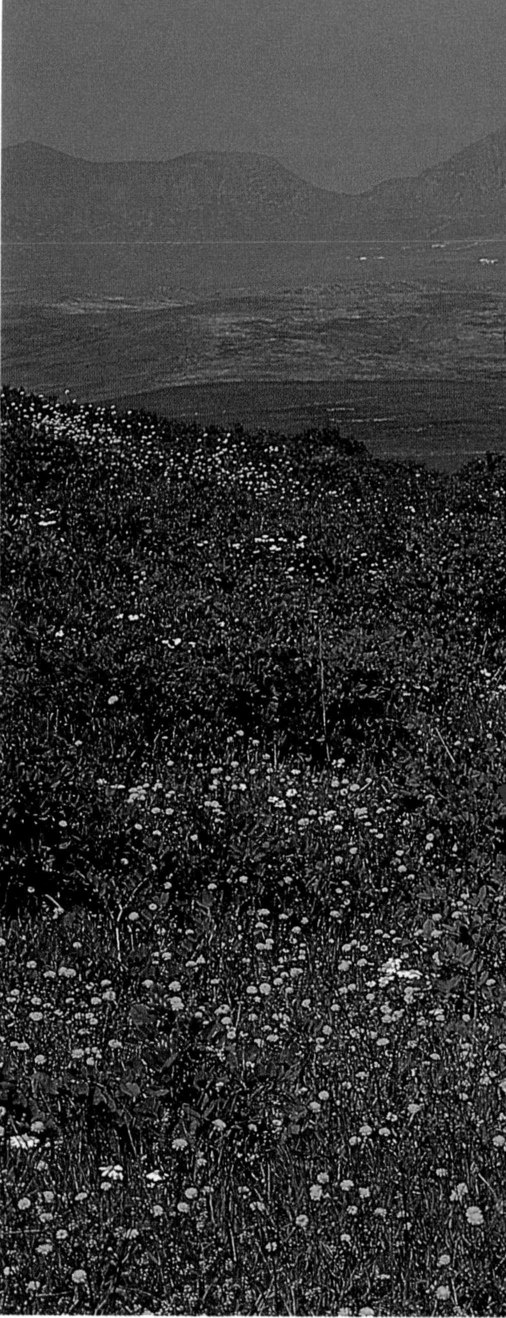

earth. Not only the colour, but also the shape, size and smell of flowers have been carefully tailored to gratify insects: a flower is the plant's way of advertising nectar as a reward for pollination. But does the bee's eye register the colours in a display of flowers in the same way that ours does? The answer is no. The bee sees the world of colour as different hues of blue, green and ultraviolet, the last of which we do not see at all. Bee blue, however, includes a range of colours that we see as pink, red, brown and cream – as well as blue. These are the flower colours that are also most attractive to bees. The red colour of the Mediterranean vetch *Hedysarum coronarium* in this photograph stands out boldly to our eyes but bees cannot see red as a distinct colour. Nevertheless they are attracted to red flowers by the ultraviolet which they radiate. 102

103. A band of yellow crown daisies *Chrysanthemum coronarium* bordering a field of spring corn appears dazzling to human and insect eyes alike. Yet both the green corn and the yellow flowers reflect the same amount of light. Only the *apparent* luminosity of yellow is greater, not the *real* luminosity. The majority of the visitors to yellow flowers are flies, bugs, beetles and small bees. Larger bees are less impressed. The round-headed, yellow daisy flower stereotype is quite unlike the favourite bee flower which is blue, pink or purple, has two lips and hides its nectaries away from thieving flies, beetles and ants at the bottom of a long corolla tube, accessible only to long-tongued insects.

104. Although we see white as a colour, physically it is a mixture of all colours, since a white surface lacks any pigment to absorb light and reflects all wavelengths to the same extent. The white flowers of cow-parsley *Anthriscus sylvestris* and hawthorn *Crataegus monogyna* shown in this photograph are both highly important suppliers of nectar in springtime Britain and northern Europe. On a sunny day, an open stand of white flowers reflects up to five times more light than even the brightest yellow flowers, such as the crown daisies in photograph **103**. The great advantage of white, therefore, as an advertisement to insects is that it increases the contrast between the flower and its background: individual white flowers stand out like beacons in an array of coloured flowers, and tree blossom becomes more highlighted against the bright sky. Indeed, blue flowers are rarely found on trees although white is common.

103

105

106

105, 106. The blue heads of globe-thistles *Echinops* stand out boldly against the monotone straw colour of the steppe grassland in which they grow in the Golan Heights between Syria and Israel (**105**). These contrast effects will be greatest to prospective pollinators of the thistle if the weather is bright and windy since a moving object has more appeal than a stationary one. Flowers growing in woodland where light levels may be only 10 per cent of those in the open field are often coloured white in order to increase contrast. The woodcock orchid *Ophrys scolopax*, also a shade-loving species, achieves contrast, not through colouring but by the bold patterning on its petals (**106**). Again, this kind of 'formal contrast' is enhanced whenever the flower moves against its background.

108

107–111. Flowers, particularly yellow, daisy-type flowers, provide rich hunting grounds for spiders such as *Misumena* whose body colour often matches that of its background. Here the use of cryptic coloration has led to the successful ambushing of a stiletto fly *Thereva* (**107**) and a small bee (**108**). But it is not unusual to find spiders lying in wait on flowers whose colours contrast conspicuously with their own (**109, 110**). Alighting insects may not necessarily see these predators, despite their vivid coloration and bold contrast, because insect vision is poor at distinguishing shapes. Success in the case of the spider shown in photograph **111** may well have been helped by the disruptive pattern of the colours on its legs and abdomen.

◀ 107

109

110

112–115. The colour adornments of insects, like those of flowers, are meant as advertisements, although the messages are different. As with flower colours, we must be careful to distinguish between what our eye sees and what the insect eye sees. But there is also a 'third eye' involved, that of the insect's predators, and this is the most important of all. The coloured tip of the wing of the male orange-tip butterfly *Anthocharis cardamines* (**112**) presumably advertises his gender to a prospective mate, and indeed butterflies, unlike bees, can see red and orange. On the other hand, the marbled patterning on the underside of the orange-tip's wing (**113**) is camouflage coloration and has been evolved to deceive the eyes of a potential predator, such as a bird. The yellow, orange and red colours of insects are usually derived from carotene, a pigment obtained from plants in the diet. The red colour of the orange-tip, however, is manufactured from proteins present in the caterpillar and pupal stages. The green markings on the underwing of *Anthocharis* are in fact an optical illusion produced by the juxtaposition of yellow and black scales, as close examination of the photograph will verify. A similar arrangement of scales producing the same effect can be seen on the underwing of the green-veined white *Artogeia napi* (**114**). Blue coloration is quite uncommon in insects and when it does occur, as in the damsel-fly *Ishnura* (**115**), it is usually caused not by pigment but by light interference. Incidentally, the tiny red globules on the body of this damsel-fly are parasitic mites attached to the soft, intersegmental membranes.

112

113

114

115 ▼

116–118. Some insects use bright or contrasting colours as a warning to potential predators that they are distasteful or possess a sting, as in the potter wasp *Delta unguiculata* (**116**) displaying characteristic yellow and black banding on its abdomen. An alternative warning colour combination, orange and black, is used by sphecid wasps and the spider-hunting pompilid wasp *Hemipepsis* (**117**). The insect shown in photograph **118** is a relatively harmless ichneumon fly which appears to be mimicking the sting-bearing sphecid *Ammophila*.

117

116

118

119. The eye-markings on butterfly wings are designed to confuse bird predators. The wall brown *Lasiommata megera* normally rests with the cryptically coloured underside of the hindwings concealing the forewings. Mating butterflies are particularly vulnerable to attacks by birds, for they are no longer capable of the usual escape reaction, a swift vertical take-off. The butterflies shown here have responded to a potential threat by sliding the tip of the forewing from behind the hindwing and exposing the eye-spots, hoping to fool the intruder.

119

121

120–122. Cryptic or concealment coloration works in two ways. If the background is plain and monotone, the best plan for the insect is to achieve a uniform matching coloration. On a more varied background, disruptive coloration in the form of mottling, streaking (**120**) or transverse banding of the legs, as seen in nymphs of the mantis *Empusa pennata* (**121**), is a more effective ploy. *Empusa* increases the effect by its stick-like appearance, due to the enormous elongation of the first thoracic segment, and the projecting turban-like crest on its head (**122**).

◀120

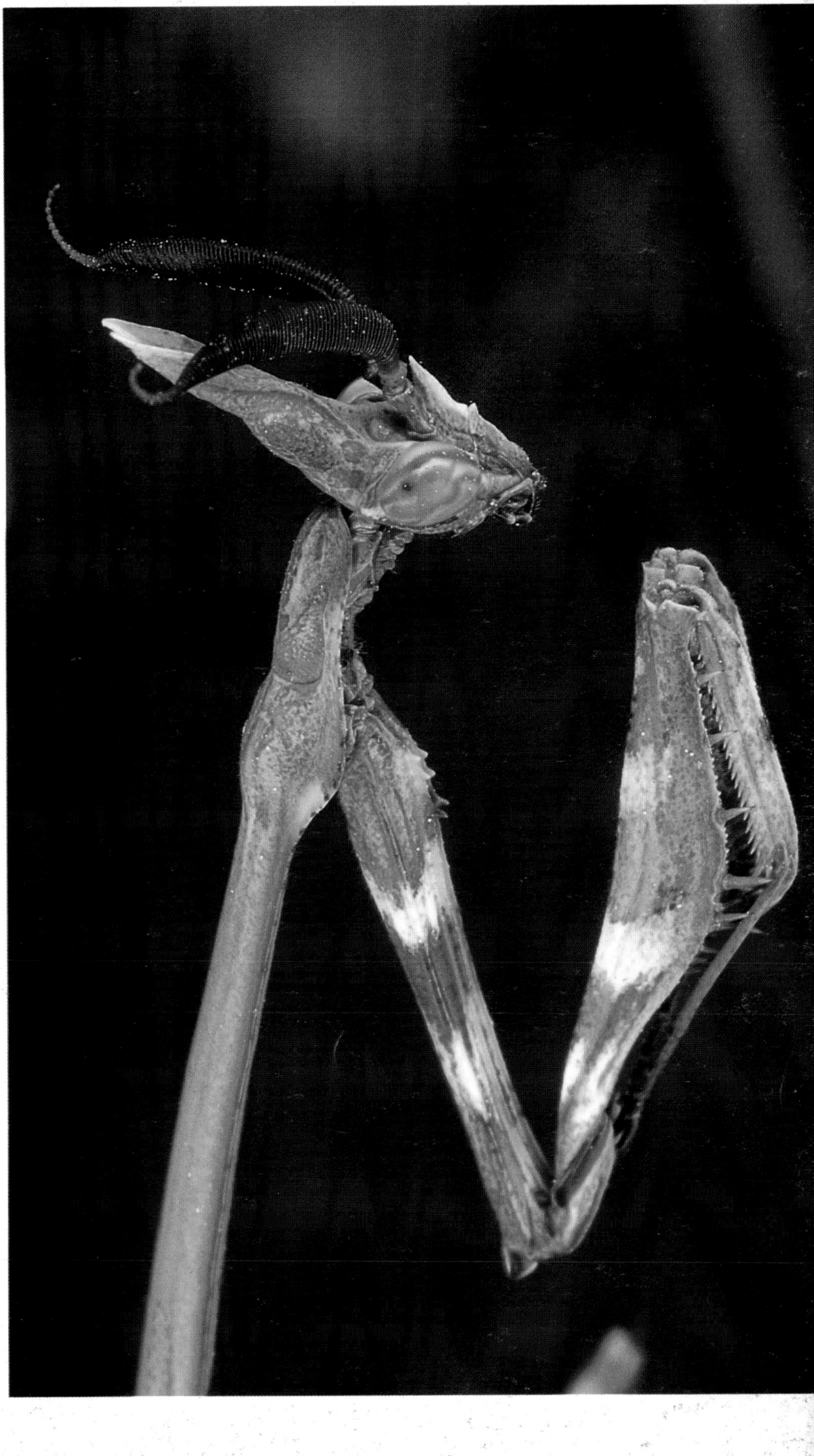

122

123. The sub-deserts south of the Moroccan Atlas mountains appear barren, monotone and waterless between the months of March and September. At first sight, this does not promise much by way of insect life, yet the presence of insectivorous birds and lizards shows that they are there, only very well camouflaged.

123

124

124, 125. Animal life in deserts, other than in the oases, tends to be concentrated around the sparse vegetation of the wadis. This environment offers little shade and the light coloration found in many desert insects not only camouflages them against predators but also maximizes the reflection of sunlight. *Eremiaphila* (**124, 125**) uses its perfect camouflage coloration to run and hunt freely over open ground, a style more reminiscent of tiger beetles than the usually indolent mantid family to which it belongs. Natural variation in body colour seems to predispose individuals to either sandy (**124**) or slaty (**125**) terrain. The jerky, stop–start movements of these insects has earned them the soubriquet 'desert tears' in the Negev desert of Israel. Although the wings are reduced and non-functional they continue to serve a useful purpose by enhancing the smooth, pebbly contour of the body.

125

126, 127. Two other desert insects, the grasshopper *Acrida bicolor* (**126**) and the mantis *Blepharopsis mendica* (**127**) use different forms of disruptive patterning. The streaky pattern of the grasshopper matches the thin grassland of the wadis and oases in which it lives whilst the transverse banding of the legs and mottling of the back of the mantis are more effective in bushy habitats.

126

127

129 ▶

128

128, 129. Form, colour and pattern are all used to good effect in the camouflage of these *Agapanthea* beetles (**128**) associated with the sparse, woody vegetation of desert wadis. Note how the extremely long antennae are carefully laid along the natural line made by the edges of the wing-cases. The pointed shape of this froghopper (**129**) lends useful camouflage amongst the thorny desert plants in which it lives.

130, 131. There are some interesting exceptions to the usual tendency towards cryptic coloration in desert insects. Brilliant golden green buprestid beetles may regularly be seen basking on tamarisk trees in the evening sunlight (**130**) and the commonest beetles in deserts, tenebrionids, are usually black (**131**). The lustrous coloration of the buprestid or 'metallic' beetles can easily be reconciled with the need to reflect unwanted heat during the daytime but the melanism of the tenebrionids is paradoxical: a black surface should absorb radiant heat rather than reflect it. The current interpretation is that melanism in these beetles promotes heat absorption in the early morning hours following the night-time chill of the desert.

131

◀ 130

4

HEAT, ENERGY AND ACTIVITY

All animals must consume energy in order to drive the cellular processes that keep them alive. This energy must be carefully budgeted in a number of different directions, for example the manufacture of new tissue for growth, physical activities such as movement and chewing, and the day-to-day maintenance of the body and all its systems. If the animal is not engaged in any physical activity at all, and has stopped growing, its energy requirements are at a minimum and are all channelled into maintenance. This is the basal metabolic rate.

BODY SIZE AND ENERGY

If we examine a range of animals, for example mammals, varying in body weight from a one-tonne (1,000,000 gram) elephant to a ten-gramme mouse and compare their basal metabolic rates, a surprising relationship emerges. You might expect that each gram of a mouse's tissue would need roughly the same amount of energy as each gram of the elephant's tissue, just to keep ticking over. This would logically mean that the whole elephant at rest would consume roughly as much energy as 100,000 resting mice. In fact, it turns out that the elephant needs only as much energy as approximately 2,000 mice. Why the fifty-fold difference between what we would expect and what we actually find?

The explanation is tied up with the geometry of the animals, combined with the fact that they are both striving to hold their body temperatures at around 40°C, not very different from our own. Regulating the body at a set temperature means that the heat coming into the body from the tissues must exactly balance the heat leaving through the skin. This is where the paradox lies. The surface area of the skin covering an animal increases with its weight, as we would expect, but not directly. In fact, mathematically speaking, surface area increases in proportion to the two-thirds power of body weight. The result is that a small animal has much more surface area across which to lose heat, relative to its body weight, than a much larger animal. In the case of the mouse, the ratio of skin area to body weight is approximately 50 times greater than it is in the elephant so, in a sense, the mouse tends to lose heat 50 times more readily than the elephant. This is why the mouse must burn up energy per gram of its tissue, at roughly 50 times the rate of the elephant. Otherwise it couldn't hold its body temperature at 40°C. Conversely, if an elephant were to burn energy at the same rate as 100,000 mice, as we originally and mistakenly guessed, its body would be grilled within minutes because it would be unable to lose heat fast enough through its skin.

THE IMPORTANCE OF SUNSHINE

This digression into the thermodynamics of mice and elephants illustrates how risky it is for an animal that is small to struggle to maintain a high body temperature, since eventually the laws of physics dictate that it will have to feed non-stop just to replace the heat being lost through its skin. This is a law of diminishing returns, quite literally, and it was probably in recognition of this fact that insects contracted out of the 'heat race' 400 million years ago when they began to evolve. Ever since, sunshine has become the vitalizing force for insects because it raises their body temperature free of charge, primes their tissues for action and allows them to channel precious energy reserves into purposeful activity rather than squandering them down an avenue of heat loss. The penalty is a decline into inactivity when the sunshine abates, although a few large moths and beetles can raise their temperature prior to flight by rapidly vibrating the flight muscles to generate internal heat. I once observed this curious shivering behaviour in, of all things, a great diving beetle *Dytiscus marginalis* which climbed out of a garden pond, propped itself up on its four front legs to catch the sunlight, then started vibrating its thorax with a distinctly audible whine. After a minute or so it ceased shivering, drew its hairy hindlegs beneath its body, leapt into the air hoping to take to flight and clattered noisily back to the ground. Another bout of shivering was followed by another hop and this time it launched successfully and flew off into the distance sounding like a large bumble-bee.

Most people associate insects with warm, sunny weather: this is when the aphids multiply in the garden and ants alarm us by filing purposefully out of cracks in the floor and the wall. Bluebottles making noisy raids from the kitchen to the living room force us to take up arms with a newspaper rolled into a bludgeon. In the evening tiny, troublesome flies are found drowning in the wine glasses. Ants in the garden are an unmitigated nuisance, defiantly tending the aphids, creating eruptions in the lawn and bringing about mysterious deaths in shrubs which they excavate, invisibly, from below.

It is a stroke of natural justice that insects benefit from sunshine because the same surface area law that forbids them from warm-bloodedness, now helps them to absorb solar heat. There is no finer exponent of this principle than that dedicated sun-bather, the butterfly. If you watch its wings as a cloud passes over the sun you will see them gently close like the pages of a book. No other insect has the butterfly's ability to use its wings as variable solar panels. Dragonflies, which rest with extended wings, can angle their bodies towards the sun and so allow the blood flowing through the hollow wing veins to carry additional heat back towards the body, but a dragonfly's wings are transparent and cannot trap radiant heat as efficiently as the butterfly's scale-covered wing.

Beetles, too, are avid sun worshippers. But they have a very good reason for not using their wings as possible solar panels. When a beetle normally prepares for take-off it has to ensure that the extension of the wings is properly synchronized with the leaping movements that the legs make. If for any reason a particular take-off attempt fails, for instance if the legs and wings get slightly out of synchrony, the beetle has to go through the whole series of motions again. The wings have to be withdrawn, neatly folded beneath their cases, and the legs have to be carefully repositioned. This is a time-consuming process, so if a beetle which already had its wings extended for the purpose of sun-bathing were confronted by a genuine emergency, such as an imminent attack by a bird, it would be fatally handicapped. However, beetles seem to manage quite well without this facility. The photograph on page 116 (**130**) shows a metallic beetle belonging to the family Buprestidae which, although mainly tropical, also occurs around the Mediterranean. This particular beetle is basking on a tamarisk tree in low, evening sunlight. In fact the metallic sheen on the buprestid's wing-cases makes the beetle a better heat reflector than a heat absorber. This is fine during the middle of the day but presents a problem in the evening when the beetle wants to absorb heat. When the sun is low in the sky I have seen buprestid beetles hanging tenuously to vegetation with the three legs of one side of the body, in order to protrude the remaining three legs and the underneath of the abdomen directly towards the sun. They will continue to hold this curious, half-suspended position even if you prod them and it evidently favours heat absorption much better than sitting with the shiny wing-cases pointing towards the sun.

Paradoxically, one of the commonest groups of desert beetles, the tenebrionids, is coloured black. This is in stark contrast to the majority of desert insects, which take on the sandy colour of their backgrounds in order to camouflage their bodies as well as to maximize heat reflection. A similar paradox seems to present itself in the case of the black bedouin goat. The melanic coloration of both of these creatures however may be an adaptation, not to heat reflection, but to heat absorption. And when does a desert animal need to absorb heat? The answer is in the early morning hours, after the cool of the desert night. This hypothesis is the one currently on offer to explain this paradox, but it is not entirely convincing. Where do desert scorpions, for instance, feature in the scheme of things since they are black or dark coloured but also active at night? No doubt interested readers will arrive at their own explanations.

STRENGTH AND MOVEMENT

Irrespective of where you stand with regard to insects, one has to admit that they have exploited the earth in which they live with some ingenuity. If sometimes this has been at our own expense we might also remember that without them life would be poorer: no flowers, a lot less fruit and vegetables, no silk and no honey. There would also be no summer swallows and virtually no bats to grace our skies. In the general equation, these bonuses must be weighed against the disease and crop destruction wrought by this, the most successful group of animals ever to evolve. Indeed insects have managed to invade almost every conceivable ecological niche, with one single, huge exception: the sea. Two-thirds of the earth's surface is strictly off-limits to them because their excretory systems simply cannot cope with the salt load.

One of the most characteristic features of insects is their small size and whereas this in general has helped them to become the successful group of animals that they are it also puts them at the mercy of certain marginal physical forces that larger animals simply ignore. Surface tension is a good example. To any insect that is not properly waterproofed against its effects, surface tension can turn a raindrop into a prison cell as the photographs on pages 132–135 (**146–149**) illustrate. The froghopper nymphs shown in the photograph on pages 134–135 (**150**) only avoid drowning in their own 'raindrop' because they secrete chemicals that reduce its surface tension and turn it into the frothy mixture that we recognize as 'cuckoo-spit'. They are then free to move about within the liquid without becoming stuck to its surface. They breathe by poking the tips of their abdomens, which are water repellent, outside the froth and exposing the openings of the tracheal tubes that conduct air to the interior of their bodies. This curious behaviour reminds us that froghoppers are close cousins of water-boatmen which also breathe by hanging from the surface of the water and taking air through the end of the abdomen into a bubble carried beneath the wing-cases.

Insects have only been able to work their way into so many different physical environments because of their ability to adapt quickly to changing circumstances, both behaviourally and physiologically. One area in which structural and functional adaptation can be seen very clearly is in the variety of different types of locomotion. To say that an animal can crawl, tunnel, jump or swim is only to beg a series of questions, because all of these activities can be done in so many different ways. The really clever trick is to be able to adapt the same basic design to achieve movement in different physical environments. For example, the larva of the lesser stag beetle *Dorcus* shown in the photograph on page 187 (**212**) manages to bore a tunnel through rotten wood using a series of peristaltic-like waves of contraction that starts at its tail and moves progressively towards its head. As the crest of the wave moves forward each segment of the body momentarily fattens and gains purchase with the solid sides of the tunnel. The segment behind then contracts, hauling the body a short distance forwards. This happens in succession up the line, so the whole body is shunted forwards with each wave. The same worm-like pattern of movement enables a caterpillar to shuffle forwards over the ground, helped in this case by up to eight pairs of feet. One of the most unusual exhibitions of peristaltic movement is provided by the legless larva of the fungus gnat shown in the photograph on page 165 (**182**), which wriggles backwards and forwards along a delicate silken tube that grips its body like an elastic stocking.

The leap of a flea or a bush-cricket presents what at first appears to be a contradiction: the feet push against the ground for only a few thousandths of a second, yet insect muscle tissue needs five or ten times as long to perform a single contraction. There is a simple explanation. The power for the initial thrust isn't coming from the muscles at all; it is coming from the explosive recoil of a spring in the legs: hence the quite astonishing velocities at which these insects catapult themselves into the air. Once triggered the spring can be cranked up again by the leg muscles, this time at a leisurely pace. The spring is formed by compressible pads of rubberized chitin at the base of the legs, or bands of elasticated material that are stretched behind the joints when the legs are folded. The tiny springtail, a primitive wingless insect, has one of the most curious jumps of all. It uses its own blood pressure to pump up its skin like a balloon. When released, the pressure forces out at high velocity a 'pogo-stick' stored beneath the end of the abdomen, causing the insect to somersault backwards.

Biological pogo-sticks are one thing, but I never expected to see a jumping maggot. This is exactly what turned up one day when I was opening a pea-pod. Inside I found, in addition to a caterpillar of the common pea moth *Cydia nigricana*, several dozen much smaller grubs only 1–2 mm in length. I could have sworn that every now and again one spat at me, like a tiny piece of shot. Placing them on a clean, flat surface and observing them with a hand lens showed what they were doing. After much strenuous and apparently purposeless wriggling, a larva would eventually succeed in doubling up its body, it would then grasp the end of its tail in its mouth, pull mightily, then suddenly release its grip and ping two or three centimetres into the air. Although I have not yet identified these tiny missiles, they bear all the hallmarks of the egregious 'cheese-skipper', the grub of a group of flies, the Piophilidae, which normally infects domestic foods.

The innumerable ways in which insects have become adapted to a life of swimming would justify a book of its own and here one can only touch on the subject. It is not unusual to find that an insect has at least two ways of swimming, one of which is quite explosive and is reserved for emergencies. Larvae of dytiscid beetles, for example, are content to paddle gently along through the water using a rhythmic beating of their legs. If alarmed, however, they will execute a sudden flick of the whole body. A similar whip-like motion, this time from side to side, will torpedo a dragonfly or damsel-fly larva forwards, helped by the expanded gills on the end of its abdomen which thrash against the water. Larval damsel-flies also use jet propulsion, squirting a stream of water from the rectum and driving themselves forwards at a velocity of half a metre a second. Many readers will be familiar with the sight of water-boatmen and diving beetles skulling themselves through the water with their highly modified hindlegs. You may be surprised to learn, however, that the insects can use these same paddles to hop into the air like grasshoppers, when they take to flight.

INSECTS: THE ULTIMATE FLYING MACHINES

Flight is arguably the insect's finest achievement in the realm of locomotion and though it shares this ability with birds and bats it owes nothing to them in terms of wing design and function. The flight apparatus of insects is unique because they wear their skeletons on the outside of their segmented bodies like suits of armour. These plates are articulated by muscle and tough, rubbery, intersegmental membrane. The wings are carried on the second and third segments of the thorax and the skeleton of these segments is rather like an orange box, minus its bottom and stood on its end. It has two sides, a base and a top. Although this 'box-section' is square, the top plate is marginally smaller than the base plate. Each wing connects to the edge of the top plate, and therefore pivots on the edge of the side plate. When the top plate is made to move rhythmically up and down, by means of muscles attached to it from the inside, the wings are automatically lowered and raised. In flight these levering movements are repeated up to several hundred times a second, depending on the species – anything less would fail to produce the aerodynamic lifting force necessary to balance the insect's weight in the air. These phenomenal wingbeat rates are far in excess of any contraction rates known to occur in active muscle. So how does the insect succeed in flying? The explanation lies in the skeletal plates. These are elastically stressed like thin sheets of metal so that when the flight muscles attached to them contract, they resonate with the plates, achieving ultra-high vibration frequencies.

Wings of course only create lift when air is moving across their surface and in order to attain a 'priming' airflow at the start of flight insects often leap into the air. It is relatively easy to measure the wingbeat-rate of an insect and the speed the wings move at. Combine these values with shape and area of the wings and the angle of attack at which they encounter the oncoming air, and then fit these data into a recognized aerodynamics formula. The result is a theoretical prediction of the amount of lift that the wings should be capable of producing. But it only works if the insect behaves like a scaled-down aircraft. And, of course, it usually doesn't. In many cases the predicted lift is too low – several times less than the insect's own body weight. So the insect must be using some tricks of its own to circumvent the laws of fixed-wing aerodynamics.

These unusual methods of lift production result from short-lived air circulations or vortices produced by interaction between the right and left wings of each pair when they come closest together at the top and bottom of the stroke. These vortices react back upon the wing surface providing extra lift and thrust. The commonest variant is the 'clap and peel' method used by butterflies and other insects with large, broad wings. The wings are clapped together above the body, then steadily peeled apart like two pages of a book. As the wings separate, a partial vacuum is formed between them and above them, which sucks in air and helps sustain the weight of the body in the air. The extra lift comes at a timely moment in the wingbeat cycle, at the top or bottom of the stroke, when the wings are almost still and unable to generate lift conventionally.

132. The material from which the exoskeleton of an insect is made, chitin, has a composite structure like fibreglass and is said to possess the tensile strength of steel. The male empid fly *Empis tessellata*, seen here, could almost be putting this claim to the test by suspending his own weight, plus that of a chunky St Mark's fly *Bibio marci*, that he has caught and is eating, by a single, extremely slender foot. This leaves five feet to manipulate the prey as he probes its body with his horny beak. *Empis* also eats plant material and can, as it were, turn its sword into a ploughshare: in photograph **29** (on page 32) an individual is using its beak to sip nectar from a flower.

132

133

133. The male *Empis tessellata* in this photograph has recently proferred a gift of a captured St Mark's fly to the female with whom it is copulating – a gesture of appeasement, perhaps, to save him from the same fate as the gift. Gift presentation takes place during nuptial flights in which a male captures an item of prey at five or six metres from the ground, offers it to the female while simultaneously seizing her in mid-air, then descends to a suitable twig from which he suspends both himself and his double payload by both of his front legs. Meanwhile he uses the middle pair of legs to support his mate's thorax and passes the hind pair carefully beneath her wings to help to manipulate the prey.

134. Copulating insects can remain engaged for many minutes or even hours and, since the genitalia disengage only with difficulty, they are especially vulnerable to attack from predators such as birds. Species that couple head-to-tail such as dragonflies and damsel-flies, or tail-to-tail such as craneflies and St Mark's flies, can still fly *in coitus*, the stronger partner determining the flight direction. In contrast, adopting the male-on-top position effectively pinions the female so that in order to make an escape the male must be able to carry her weight as well as his own, as we see in this photograph of the dung-fly *Scatophaga*.

134

135

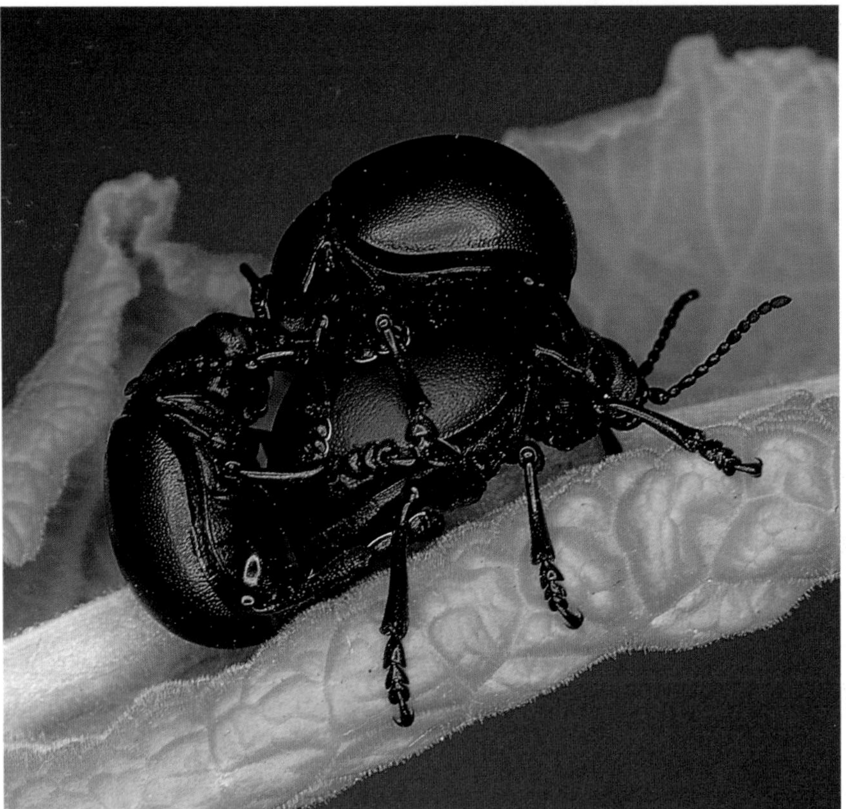

136

135, 136. The feet of the beetle *Oxythyrea* are long and slender, terminating in a pair of claws, and are perfectly adapted for anchoring the insect on to the flower-heads on which it feeds. Such flexible 'grappling hooks', however, are rather less effective tools when it comes to preventing the male from being dislodged from the female's back during copulation (**135**). At such times he presents a picture of a rather heavy sac languidly slung across her shoulder. The bloody-nosed beetle *Timarcha tenebricosa* (**136**) avoids this potential hazard by having broad, flat feet covered with a brush of minute, hooked hairs. Behaving like the fabric 'Velcro', these brushes can engage even the tiniest crevices in apparently smooth surfaces, enabling the male for instance to cling limpet-like to the wing-cases of the female.

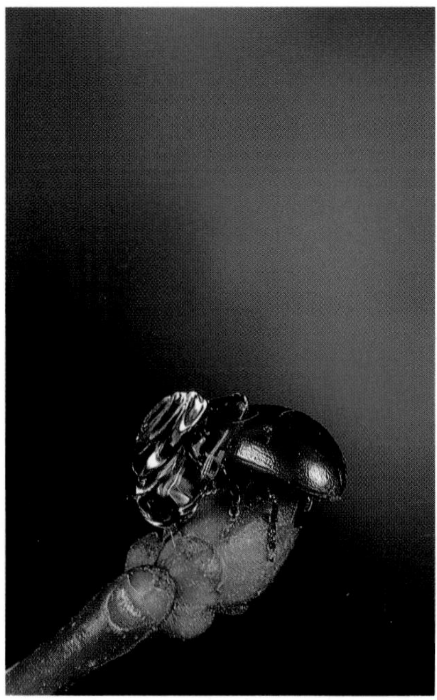

138

137, 138. The adhesive power of the feet of the chrysomelid beetle *Chrysolina* is put to the test by a raindrop. A falling water droplet (**137**) can produce a momentary force on impact of up to half an atmosphere. As the surface tension film of the droplet moulds itself around the beetle's smooth carapace (**138**), the insect's feet withstand the test and it remains undislodged.

137

139

139. Caterpillars are equipped with two types of leg, the true legs on the thorax, which are equivalent to those of the adult butterfly, and 'false' legs, or pro-legs, on the abdomen. The maximum number of pro-legs is five pairs, the two at the end of the body being modified as claspers. Each pair of pro-legs can be independently telescoped into or out of the body: fluid pressure from the body forces it out and special retractor muscles attached to the middle of the cup-like sole of the foot pull it in. The circle of tiny hooks, or crochets around the sole is used to latch on to rough surfaces, but if the sole is planted on to a smooth surface and the retractor muscle is contracted, a vacuum is created and the foot serves as a sucker.

140, 141. Caterpillar pro-legs are especially effective for clinging to long, narrow objects like grass stems, since then each pair is able to grip in a 'finger-and-thumb' manner (**140**). This tiger-moth caterpillar (**141**) demonstrates the flexibility of its pro-legs, using the claspers to grip independently of the other four pairs. The curious nipple-like spinnerets on the cheeks are used to construct a silken cocoon before pupation, but tent moths can also use them to spin out a life-line when they hurriedly drop out of their tents when alarmed.

140

141 ▶

142

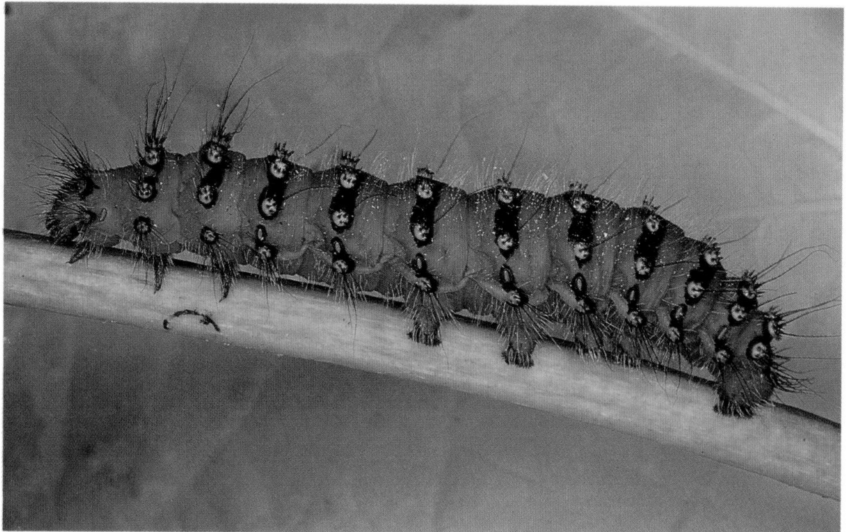

143

144

142–145. As a caterpillar moves forward, a rippling wave can be seen travelling from its tail to its head. The faster the wave, the faster the movement of the caterpillar. The wave results from each segment of the body in turn being telescoped into the segment in front. Beginning at the tail segment, the claspers are raised, the segment is telescoped forwards, and the claspers are put down again. This sequence is then repeated up the line so that the body is shunted forwards like a series of railway carriages.

We can see this happening in the caterpillar of the emperor moth *Saturnia pavonia* in photographs **142**, **143** and **144**, which are in sequence. In the first photograph the claspers have just been drawn forwards by the telescoping of segments 10–7. The pro-legs of segments 6–3 are still in contact with the ground. In the next photograph (**143**) the wave of contraction has moved forwards to segments 6 and 5; the corresponding pro-legs have been raised and are being drawn a 'step' forwards. Finally, in the last photograph (**144**) the contractile wave has advanced to segments 4 and 3. Meanwhile the pro-legs of segments 6 and 5 have again been put down on the ground.

From this sequence we see that each full 'stride' taken by the body comprises five 'mini-strides' taken one after the other by the pro-legs, followed by three more mini-strides taken by the true legs. Some caterpillars, such as that of the Silver Y moth *Autographa gamma* (**145**) have only three pairs of pro-legs, leaving a large unsupported gap between the true legs and the first of the abdominal pro-legs. This tendency to reduction in the number of pro-legs reaches its extreme in caterpillars of geometrid moths, known as loopers, which have only one pair of pro-legs in addition to the

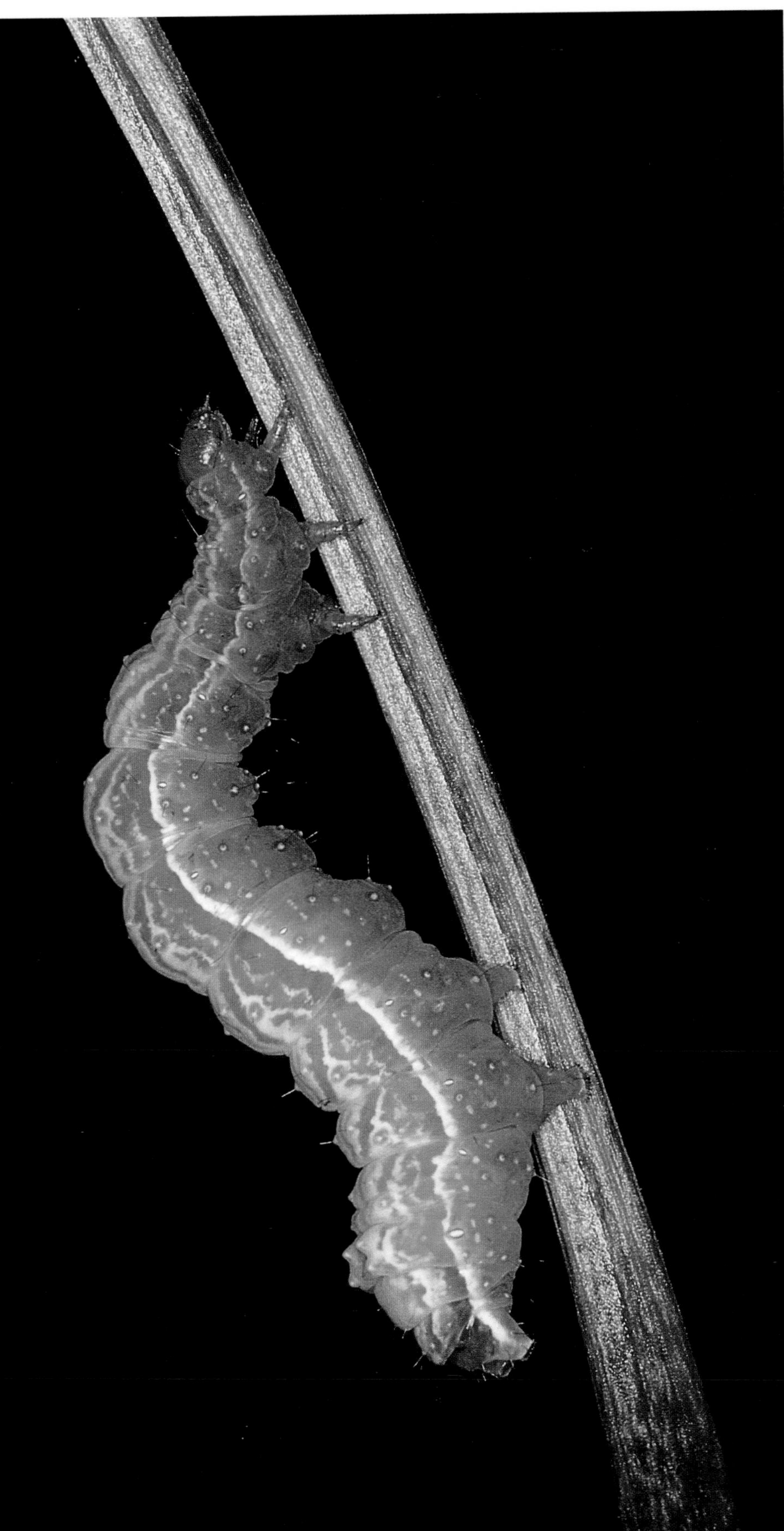

145

claspers and this allows them to arch their bodies into loops as they move. Although this method obviously economizes on strides, it appears to incur a penalty in terms of speed, since loopers in general are not nearly as fast as 'shuttlers' that have kept the full complement of pro-legs.

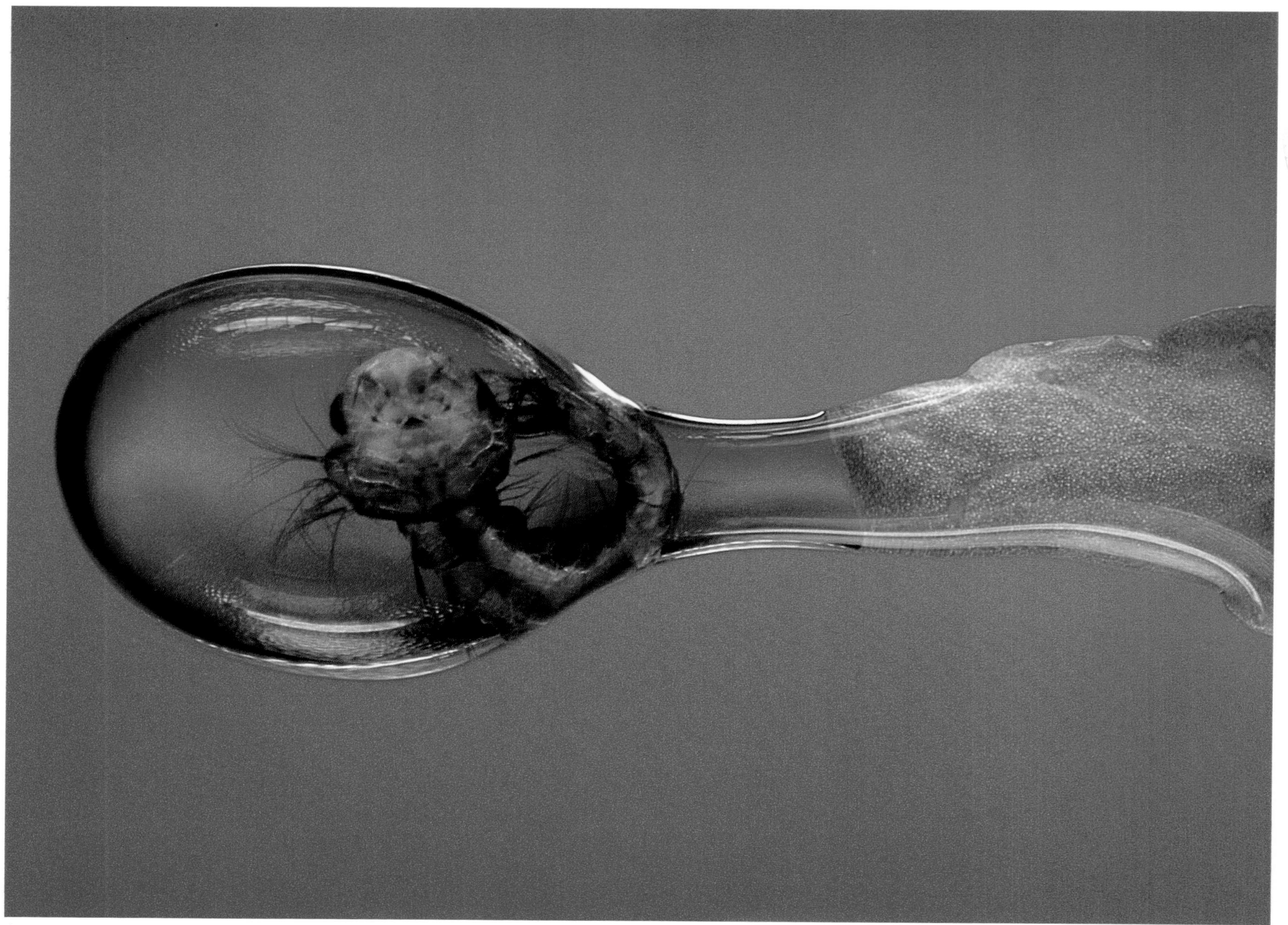

146

146, 147. A small insect can be inordinately affected by insignificant physical forces like the surface tension of water. A measure of these effects can be gained simply by looking at the formation of a water droplet on a leaf. Just before such a droplet detaches (**146**), the elastic force of the surface film around it exactly equals the weight of the water. Little wonder that a midge larva which accidentally wriggles into such a droplet, and whose weight is only a fraction of that of the water enclosed, finds itself completely imprisoned within its walls (**147**).

147

148–150. A tiny leaf-hopper is trapped by its wings within the surface tension film of a raindrop (**148**). Presented with a foothold, the insect can drag itself free, using the full strength of its muscles (**149**). Ironically, nymphs of the very closely related froghopper (**150**) develop inside, and are absolutely dependent on, a large water droplet. They are able to move freely within the droplet only because of the presence of surfactant chemicals which lower its surface tension and turn it into a frothy mixture. The common names 'spittle bug' and 'cuckoo-spit insects' are entirely apt, since mucus from the human lung contains a very similar surfactant that prevents the moist linings of the lungs from sticking together under their own surface tension.

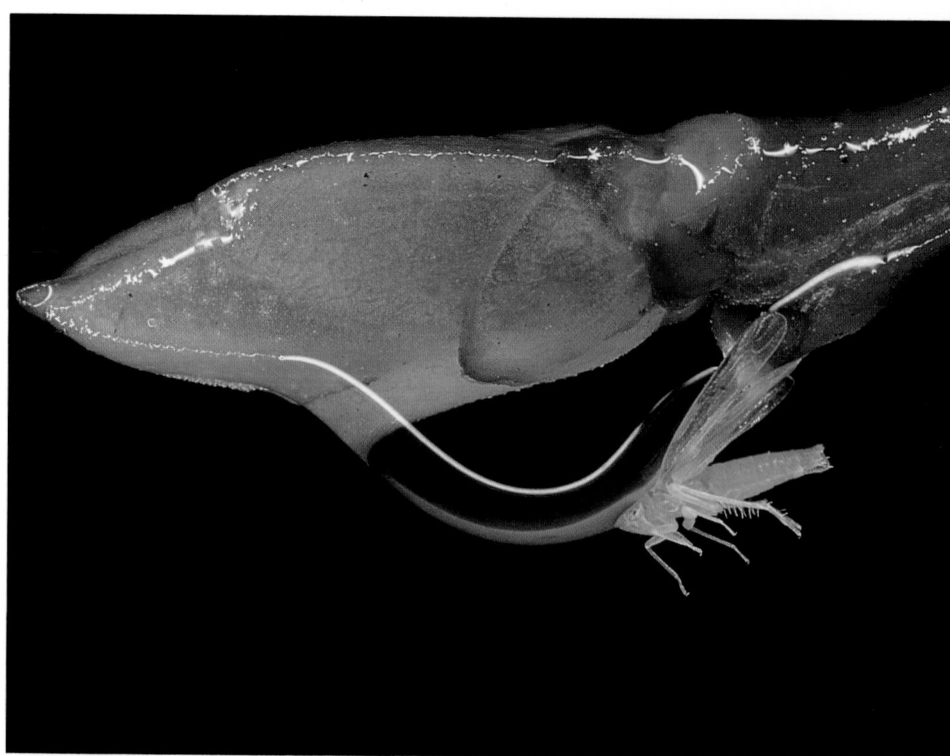

148

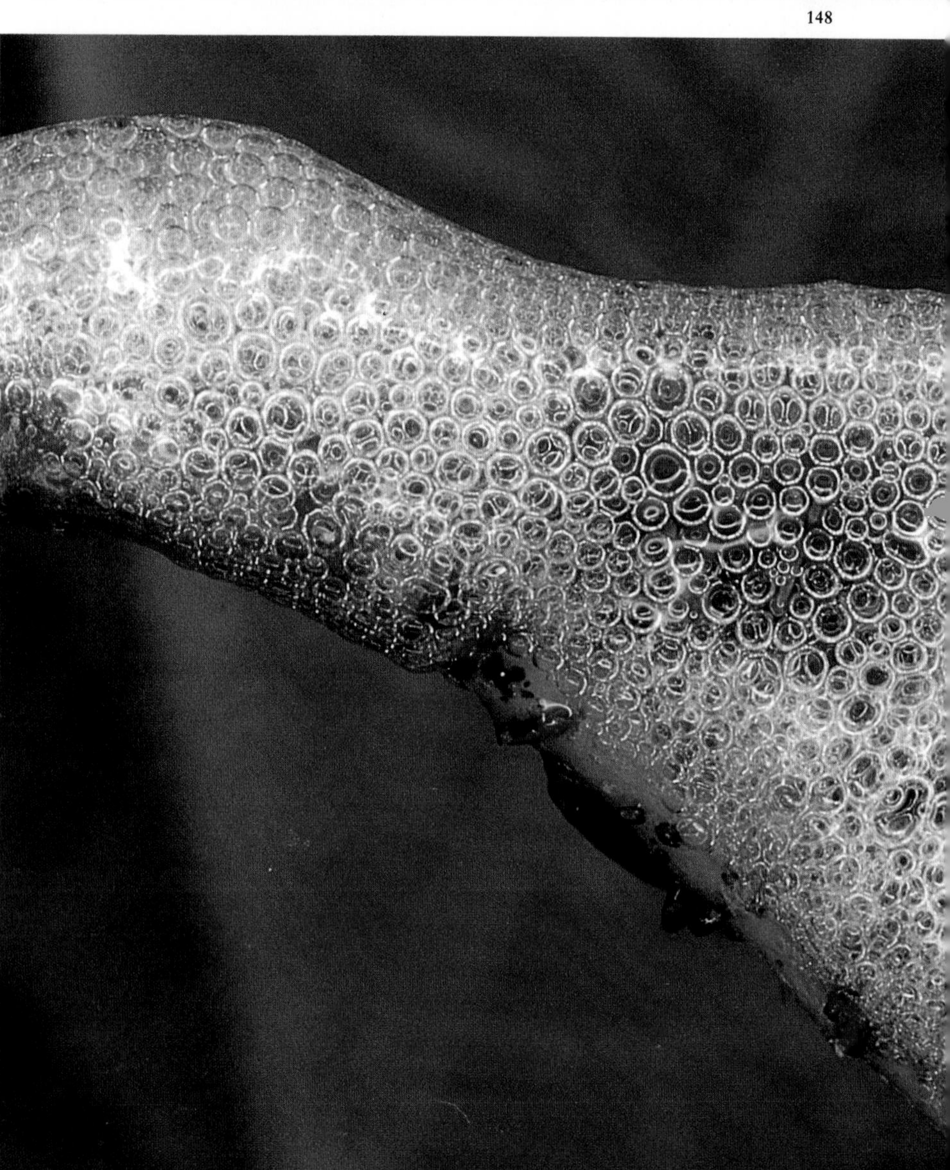

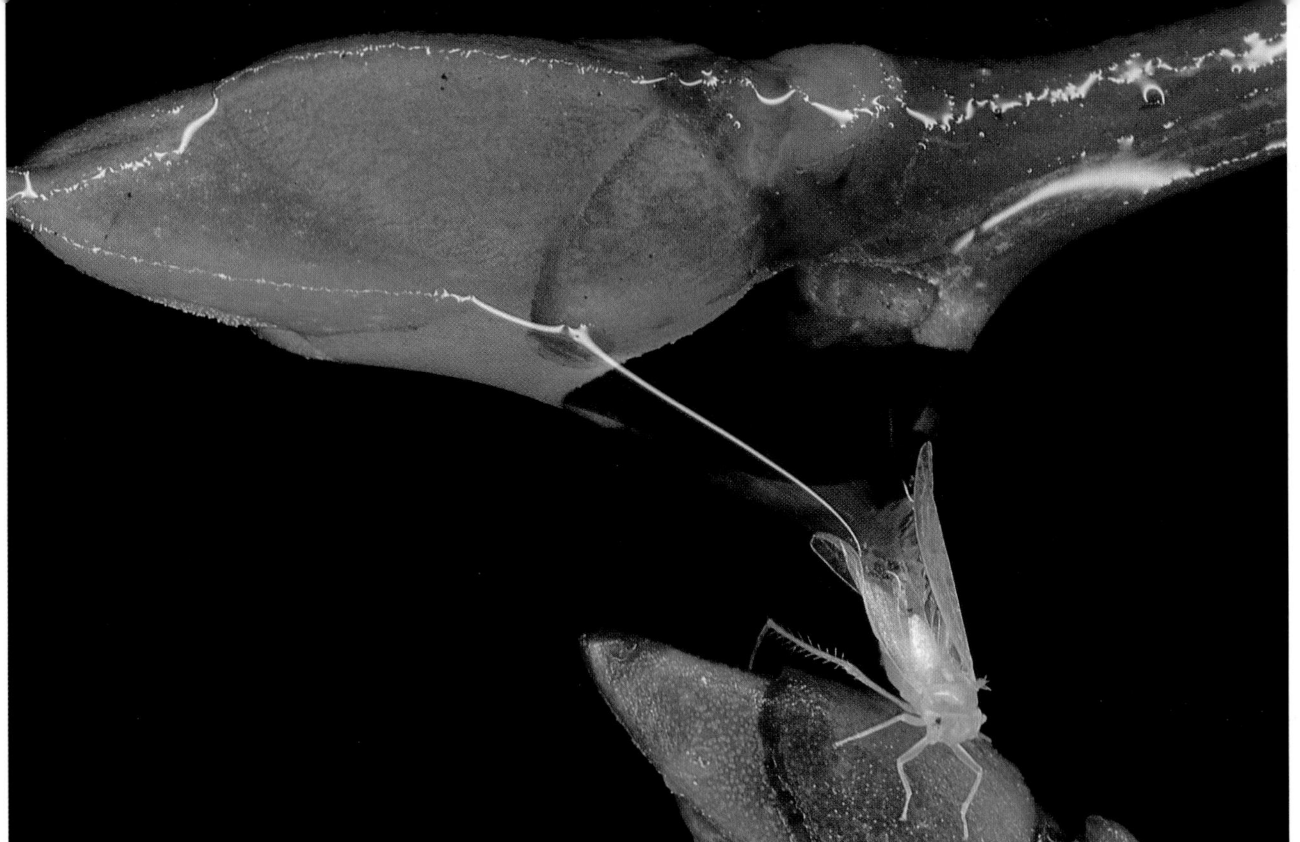

149

150

151, 152. Even airborne insects may not entirely escape the effects of surface tension if, that is, they happen to be flying in the rain. A raindrop is surrounded by an elastic envelope and when it encounters a small suspended object like a flying insect, it behaves like a balloon full of water. If it collides directly with the insect, instead of breaking up into smaller droplets and dissipating its energy in this way, it sloshes about within the envelope and transfers most of its impact to the insect. The effect is rather like being hit with a beach-ball filled with water as opposed to receiving the same amount of water thrown from a bucket. Fortunately, from the insect's point of view, the statistical likelihood of receiving a full-frontal blow from a raindrop is quite small. More likely, as in the flying wasp *Vespula vulgaris* shown here (**151, 152**), a glancing blow will produce a temporary loss of control, without knocking the insect to the ground.

◀ 151 152

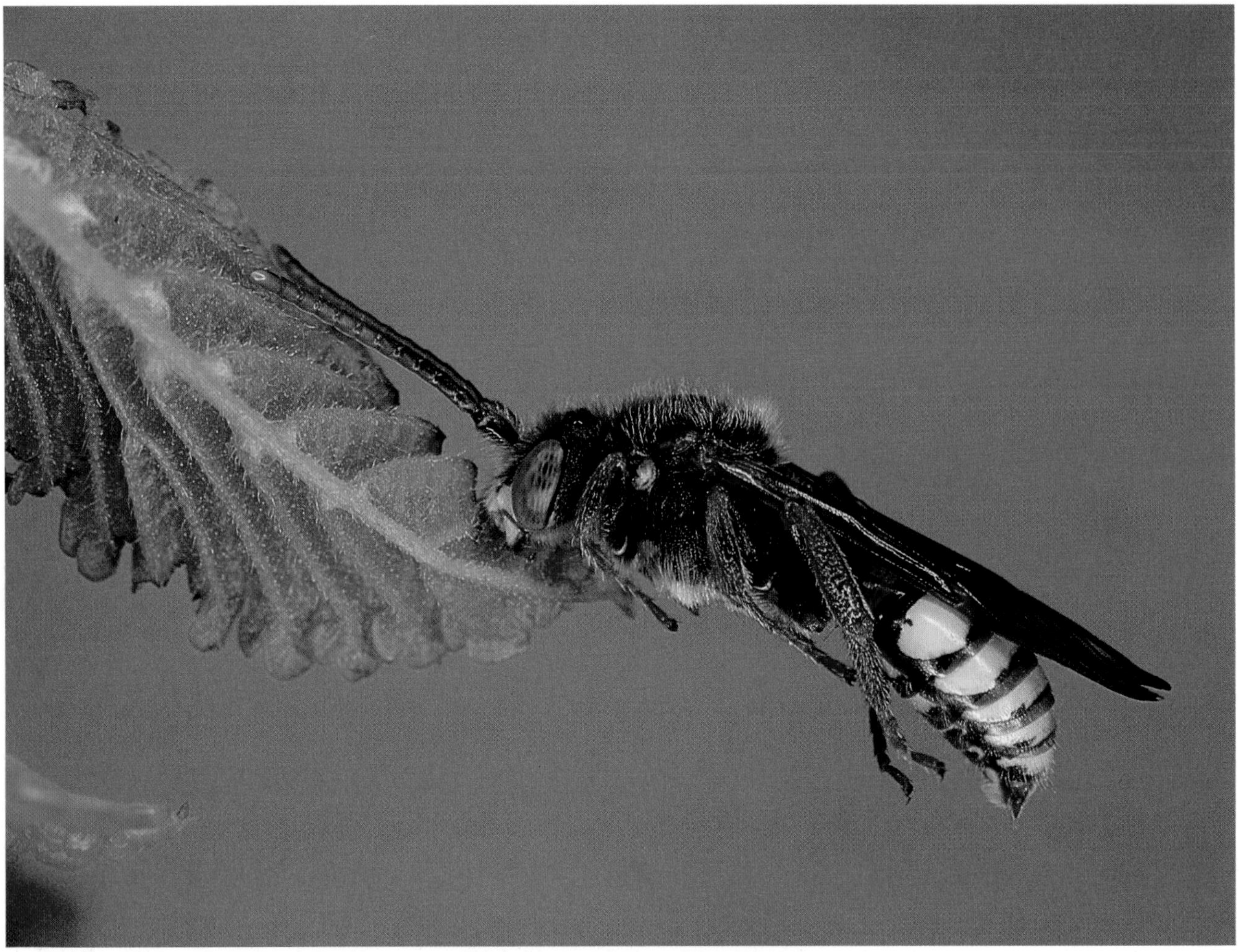

153

153–155. It remains an enigma why certain wasps suspend their bodies by their jaws when roosting. The solitary wasp *Nomada* (**153**) can often be found so engaged just before nightfall in springtime and early summer. The evanioid wasp and the vespid wasp shown in photographs **154** and **155** respectively have not entirely taken the weight off their feet: could it be that the jaw-hold provides just that extra element of security if the wasp slips too deeply into slumber . . . ?

155

154 ▶

156. The crystalline transparency of insect wings is due to their extreme thinness, yet despite this they possess remarkable strength and resilience. The delicacy of appearance of the wings of the lacewing is self-evident from the insect's name, but the complex network of veins running through them provides strength without sacrificing flexibility. Note how the veins of the locust wings in the foreground of this photograph radiate like spokes into the membranes and are interconnected by a complex web of subsidiary veins.

158

157, 158. Although many species of earwig have highly developed wings, few ever use them and certainly not the common *Forficula auricularia* (**157**). The tiny *Labia minor* seen in photograph **158** is an exception and it may occasionally be seen rising gently into the air on still summer evenings, along with a host of other insects also in the act of dispersing. *Labia* beautifully exemplifies the main principles of wing design: a stiff leading edge formed by the coalescence of a number of individual veins, and a vane which is supported, fan-like, by radiating spokes.

◀ 156

157

159

159, 160. The forewings of a locust are leathery and strap-like and are less important in generating lift during flight than the much more voluminous hindwings. The radiating veins of the hindwing support its membrane like the struts of an umbrella (**159**). This arrangement also allows the wing to be folded and unfolded quickly like a lady's fan. This photograph of an Egyptian grasshopper *Anacridium aegyptium* leaping into flight (**160**) gives a good impression of the fan-wise opening of the wing as it is raised from its resting position over the abdomen.

160

161, 162. Many long-legged leaping insects such as grasshoppers and locusts, and the long-horned bush-crickets shown in photographs **161** and **162**, are also good fliers. They use the power and speed of the leap to prime the airflow across the wings and so hasten the aerodynamic process.

161

163–165. One advantage of large, sail-like wings is that they can be beaten quite slowly and economically, at say 20 or 30 strokes per second, and yet still produce enough lift to sustain the weight of the body in the air. Another advantage is that their flexibility allows an interaction to occur between the left and right wings of a pair when they come together at the top and bottom of the stroke. This sequence of three photographs of a flying bush-cricket *Phaneroptera* shows how the hind-wings peel apart at the beginning of the downstroke. Peeling causes a vacuum to form between the wings which helps to produce more lift.

163

164

165

166

166. Although stick insects are generally sedentary, not to say comatose, creatures, many have well-developed hindwings and are capable of flight over short distances if provoked. This flying pink-winged stick insect displays the same peeling of the wings that we saw in the flying bush-cricket in the previous photograph. The forewings can just be recognized in this specimen as tiny rudimentary flaps in front of the base of the hindwings.

167, 168. The hardened wing-cases or elytra of beetles are modified forewings whose main role is to enclose and protect the more delicate hindwings when they are not being used. During flight, the elytra are usually held in a V-shape directly above and at right-angles to the body, as in this metallic beetle *Julodis* (**167**). In this position they are safe from any physical interference from the beating of the hindwings, but at the same time they

168

can produce a modicum of passive lift as the beetle is driven forwards through the air. The sexton beetle *Necrophorus humator* (**168**) proves the exception that tests the rule because it positions its upturned elytra roof-wise exactly between the bases of the beating forewings. The reason for the departure from convention is not clear, although the forewings may possibly benefit by being able to peel against the smooth surfaces of the inverted wing-cases.

167

169

170

171

169. True bugs belonging to the sub-order Heteroptera have fore and hindwings that are physically coupled together and behave as a single lifting surface during flight. The coupling apparatus consists of a row of hooks along the leading edge of the hindwing that engages a groove on the trailing edge of the forewing. In this photogaph of a flying assassin bug, *Rhinocoris iracundus*, recognizable by the fearsome-looking 'beak' with which it impales its victims, the line of attachment between the two wings can be clearly seen.

170, 171. During flight the main veins in the wing can bend under pressure like elastic rods, although this bending is usually confined to the upstroke phase of the beat. Apart from protecting the wing from excessive stresses, one-way bending allows subtle changes in wing shape and wing profile which may improve aerodynamic performance. In these photographs a brown lacewing (170) and a click beetle (171) are being viewed directly from above and from below the body respectively. These angles allow us to see how the wings have been forced to bend downwards, indicating that they must be in the middle of the upstroke. If they had been photographed in the equivalent position in the middle of the downstroke, there would have been no sign of bending.

172. Green lacewings have two pairs of wings but, unlike those of true bugs, each pair beats independently and out of phase with the other. In this photograph both wing pairs are at the top of their stroke and are approximately in synchrony. A glance at the lacewing in photographs **156** and **170** however, in which the wings are positioned at the beginning of the upstroke, shows that during this phase of the beat the forewings are moving in advance of the hindwings.

173

173. Plume moths have highly unusual wings in that they are divided into a number of feather-like segments, each consisting of a fringe of hairs arranged around a main longitudinal vein. The result is an extremely lightweight wing design which loses none of the lift-generating powers of its solid counterpart because the air continues to flow across the tightly spaced hairs, and not between them.

5

THE END OF AN INSECT'S YEAR

THE RETREAT INTO AUTUMN

When we think of autumn most of us conjure up an image of falling leaves and indeed autumn in North America is colloquially known as 'the fall'. Autumnal leaf fall, however, is essentially a feature of temperate climates, where there is a strong seasonal temperature variation from warm summers to cold winters. In the far north and on high ground further south, evergreen, coniferous forests predominate whereas further south, in the sub-tropics and tropics, temperatures remain high all the year round and even deciduous trees tend to keep their leaves much longer and do not shed them all at the same time.

Leaf-fall of course is just one aspect of a general winding down of the biological world in preparation for a prolonged season of extremely low level, or survival, activity. Metereological and biological events in autumn do not always seem to keep in step. It is not unusual to experience in Britain and northern Europe spells of settled, sunny weather in October associated with a lingering pattern of summer-like anticyclones. The same clear skies, however, bring frosty nights and it is these that explain the curious absence of insects enjoying the 'Indian summer' in the same way as we ourselves are doing.

Shrinking daylength and falling shade temperatures affect insects both directly, through a slowing down of their own physiological activities, and indirectly by suppressing plant growth and removing the insects' primary source of food. Any plants remaining in flower in September and October become a mecca for nectar-hungry insects. On sunny autumn days flowering ivy becomes practically covered in a seething mass of greenbottles, bluebottles, drone-flies, wasps and red admiral butterflies. The sea-lettuce *Eryngium* fulfils a similar role on the otherwise baked and impoverished slopes of the mountains of southern Europe.

In late summer and autumn, the straw-coloured pastures of the deep south of Spain boast but a single flower in bloom, that of the yellow, beacon-like ragwort *Senecio*, detested by cattle but supporting a microcosm of insect life. The last of the scoliid wasps *Scolia hirta* visit it for nectar; grasshoppers, crickets and small dictyopharid leaf-hoppers benefit from its shelter; and the mantids *Mantis religiosa*, *Iris oratoria*, *Ameles spallanziana* and *Empusa pennata* all use its green, leafy stems as a lair.

Autumn insects fall generally into two categories: those that are programmed to die and those that are programmed to survive. In botanical parlance these are the 'annuals' and the hardy 'perennials', although even the perennials are unlikely to survive more than one winter. By the time the first autumn frosts arrive the hardy insects have already been heeding the signs and making adjustments to their behaviour and their physiology. Survival means finding shelter and those with the appropriate instinct will have crawled into nooks and crannies inside dead vegetation or under stones, anywhere that promises to be rainproof and windproof. Others will have taken out greater insurance against the weather by constructing hibernation nests to their own requirements.

For those lacking the survival instinct, death comes quickly by starvation or exposure. The remaining energy reserves of stoneflies, mayflies, scorpion-flies, craneflies, drone-flies, damsel-flies, moths and any solitary bees and wasps are soon drained to a level where they can no longer resist the cold. Those that are going to perish evidently perish easily and it is quite ironic to see large specimens of dragonflies, bush-crickets and grasshoppers, all apparently in pristine condition, knowing that within a few days they will all have disappeared. From a strictly biological viewpoint this does not present a paradox since they have fulfilled their genetic potential. Their offspring are already in the making, in the form of eggs, larvae or pupae which, unlike their parents, are programmed to survive the winter. These cold-intolerant species of insect can also be viewed as being victims of their own physiological narrowness. The various species of locust, cricket and grasshopper that are native to southern Europe and North Africa only really feel comfortable in air temperatures of between 30 and 40°C and they strive to preserve their own body temperature in the middle of this range by dipping into shade or sun-bathing, as required. So, although a scattering of these insects may survive a mild winter, the majority will be unable to forage and hence keep themselves alive even at temperatures of 10 or 15°C.

Insect blood freezes well below 0°C on account of the presence of sodium, potassium and chloride ions which lower its freezing point. This fortuitous property of blood may increase the chances of survival in freezing weather but only if the insect has already built up its energy reserves. True hibernators automatically become hyperphagic as winter approaches and some will broaden their diet to encompass almost anything that is edible. In autumn the common wasp *Vespula vulgaris* becomes a regular sight not only around the proverbial jam-pot, and the windfall apples, but also on the flowering ivy. If you watch it scuttling across the blossom, you will see that it is not only sipping nectar, but also snatching up any small insects that come within reach and dispatching them greedily between its toothed mandibles.

Autumn is not without its special benefits to insects, at least for a short time. Fungal specialists reach their zenith: for example, fungus beetles (Mycetophagidae), fungus gnats (Mycetophilidae) and the colourful rove beetle *Oxyporus* seen in the photograph on page 164 (**180**). The mildew-feeding ladybirds *Micraspis 16-punctata* and *Thea 22-punctata* are also given an opportunity to stoke up reserves for their winter hibernation. Windfall orchard fruits such as apples, pears and plums and their hedgerow equivalents, crab-apple and sloe, offer a welcome source of sugar to butterflies, moths, common wasps and, especially when the fruit has begun to ferment, fruit-flies (Drosophilidae). Weevil larvae fatten on acorns, hazelnuts and the pips of fleshy fruits, and the larvae of certain gall-producing wasps (Cynipidae) and flies (Tephritidae) begin to develop in a wide variety of galls afflicting oak and willow trees and the stems and heads of thistles. Adult gall-wasps and gall-flies will emerge the following spring, having been protected against snow, ice and rain by the corky tissue of the gall.

SURVIVING THE WINTER

In the depths of a cold winter, with the soil turned in the words of the Christmas carol, 'hard as iron' and the water frozen 'like a stone', anyone who happened to be outdoors would probably have neither the time nor the inclination to reflect on the fate of insects. On such days it is easy to arrive at the conclusion that all insects are dead and that somehow the butterflies, aphids and bumble-bees that arrive in the gardens next year will do so miraculously by a process of spontaneous generation. Even if one does find the motivation to abandon the warm fireside and venture into the field, it is quite difficult at first to convince yourself that there are any insects alive out there.

But there are signs, even as you cross the threshold, and especially if the sky happens to contain a glimmer of watery sunlight. You may notice a column of winter gnats dancing in a still corner of the garden, or hear the unseasonal buzzing of a honey-bee lured out, despite the cold, by the scent of winter-flowering *Mahonia* or *Viburnum*. A drab-coloured winter moth *Operophtera brumata* may be seen clinging to the outside of the window-pane whilst inside, sensing the sun's rays streaming into the normally dim-lit room, a green lacewing or a small tortoiseshell butterfly crawls out on to the curtains. Upon the south-facing garden wall a lone bluebottle lethargically suns itself: your leg brushes against an evergreen shrub and flushes out a plume moth which flutters a short distance to the shelter of the next shrub.

These are a few of winter's 'light-sleepers', casual hibernators which, as a rule, seek out a conveniently dry spot in which to spend the winter but remain alert to the possibility of a freak succession of warmer days that might offer opportunities to forage for food. However, they are merely the tip of a much larger and more conservative body of insects that regularly hibernate but remain hidden to the casual eye, aware that one sunny day does not make a summer. Only a prolonged increase in air temperature, coupled with a steady increase in daylength, can break the much deeper hibernation instinct of these insects, and release the desire to disperse, forage and eventually find a mate.

If you want to find winter insects, ponds and streams are the best places to start looking for them. The majority of these are not hibernating in the strict sense; they are the larvae of dragonflies, damsel-flies, alder flies, caddis flies and stoneflies which continue to grow and develop through the winter, cocooned from the worst excesses of the weather above. Scooping pond water in mid-January might not strike you as a worthwhile sacrifice for the investment in knowledge. Try instead sifting through soil and leaflitter, or better still carefully excavating dead tree stumps with a pocket-knife. This will require just as much if not more patience, but will avoid painfully frozen fingers and, moreover, will present you with an opportunity to discover some of the finest exponents of the art of winter survival.

The photograph on page 184 (**208**) shows a hibernating queen hornet *Vespa crabro*, the largest of the European social wasps. Although many people claim to have seen hornets, these insects are in fact quite shy and elusive and are more likely to be found in woodland than in towns and open fields. I suspect that when people say 'hornet', they often mean any large wasp such as the queens of *Vespula germanica* or *Vespula vulgaris*. At any rate, I was never fortunate enough to see a hornet myself until I unexpectedly came across one asleep in mid-winter. Now that I know where and how they hibernate, I feel confident that I can go outdoors on any winter's day and find at least two or three specimens, although they continue to elude me in summertime.

When she prepares to hibernate, a queen hornet first of all locates a suitably rotted, fallen tree stump in old woodland. Not any old tree stump will do. It needs to be covered with thick bark which has already separated away from the underlying wood, but is itself still intact and cannot easily be breached from the outside by snow, rain and frost. Dead oak, ash, elm and pine are ideal; sycamore, beech, hornbeam and lime all have a thin bark which easily peels, and is far less serviceable, not only to queen hornets, but also to most of their co-hibernators. Having selected a log, the hornet now begins to scoop out a chamber in the debris of soil and half-digested wood just beneath the bark. She carefully avoids the upper surface of the log, which catches the worst of the weather, and concentrates on the flanks where the drainage is better and the debris remains moist but not sodden. The chamber is scooped out with legs and jaws and is constructed so that it is larger than her body; this allows for expansion of the surrounding debris, if it becomes frozen, and saves her from being crushed between the contracting walls of her own cell. Her task of excavation has been made easier by the fact that the wood-eating larvae of certain beetles and craneflies have reduced the surface wood of the log to a soft, crumbly texture.

When she is satisfied that the cell is complete, she pulls her antennae down over her face, folds each of her wings lengthwise along a special crease designed for the purpose and tucks them out of harm's way underneath her body. In this position, evoking a curious reversion to her own pupal state, she prepares to ride out the long winter ahead. Side by side with her in this vigil are other insects that have prepared themselves in a similar manner. Bumble-bees, carrion beetles (*Silpha*), female earwigs carefully shrouding their eggs with their own bodies, and fat caterpillars of noctuid moths may all be found in the same log as the queen hornet, each in their own custom-made hibernation cells.

The cracked and brittle stems of hogweed *Heracleum sphondylium* and various thistles offer refuge for any insects small enough to creep inside their hollow interiors, while the dead heads of thistles, knapweeds, teasels, hawkweeds and burdocks play host to a variety of specialized larvae which have induced the plant to form tough, weather-resistant galls around them. To the casual eye, these strewn pieces of vegetation are no more than the debris of the previous summer, but to many of our commoner insects they offer a simple ark to convey them through the most perilous season.

174–176. The autumnal colours of beech leaves (**174**) may evoke the mellowness of the season but they also signify the final withdrawal of any nutrients that might be useful to browsing insects. A queen wasp basks in the clear, sloping sunlight typical of the shortening days (**175**) but within weeks it will have found a cool, dry place in which to hibernate under the dead bark of a tree, sometimes suspending itself vertically by its jaws (**176**).

174

176

175

177. The sight of a ploughed autumn field is a reminder that many insect larvae and pupae will endeavour to ride out the harshness of winter buried in the soil beneath herbage and grass tussocks. Some of these are serious pests including the larvae of click beetles (wireworms), craneflies (leather-jackets) and swift and noctuid moths. Ploughing normally gets rid of these and they will probably benefit from the farming practice of 'set-aside', in which fields are allowed to lie fallow, without crops.

177

178–179. The majority of adult insects still left alive by the time autumn arrives will die anyway, from starvation, the increasing cold or fungal and bacterial infection. For those remaining, the chances of surviving the winter ahead depends on their ability to build up sufficient energy reserves. For those heavily reliant on nectar as an energy source, fewer and fewer plants are left in blossom, so the occasional late-flowerer like ivy *Hedera ilex* (**178**) comes as a benediction. The red admiral *Vanessa atalanta* (**179**), comma *Polygonia c-album*, peacock *Inachis io*, small tortoiseshell *Aglais urticae* and brimstone butterflies *Gonepteryx rhamni* will be joined by bluebottles, greenbottles, social wasps and the last of the summer hoverflies, all jostling for a final share of the bounty.

179 ▼

178

180

182

180–182. Whilst autumn offers lean fare for most insects, for some it brings a resurgence of life. Rotting fruit provides a welcome alternative to nectar for moths and butterflies and even fermenting fruit has its own mildly alcoholic connoisseurs in the tiny fruit-flies or drosophilids. Insects that eat, breed or simply hunt for other insects inside bracket fungi and toadstools now reach their zenith, including fungus beetles (Mycetophagidae), fungus midges (Mycetophilidae) and the rove beetle *Oxyporus rufus* (**180**) found inside toadstools (**181**). Some species of fungus gnat browse on tiny mildews, fungi and algae growing on rotten wood stumps, wriggling back and forth along silken tubes (**182**). Mildews provide the staple for 16-spot and 22-spot ladybirds *Micraspis 16-punctata* and *Thea 22-punctata*, which will soon be retreating into hibernation.

181

183

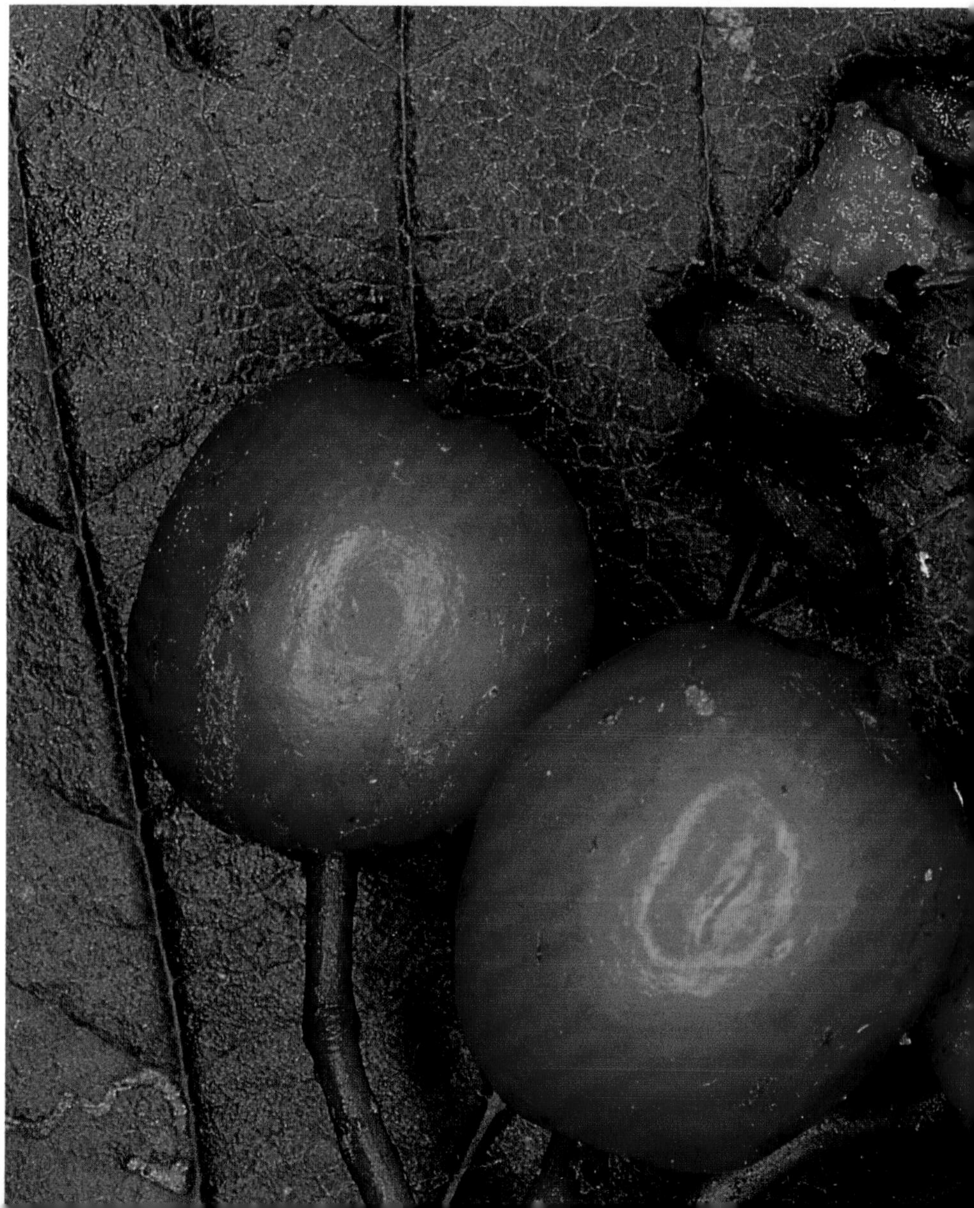

183–185. Apples are tunnelled by insect larvae such as the caterpillar of the codlin moth, *Cydia pomonella*, and seeds have their own specialists, including beetle larvae living inside acorns (**183**) and the pips of whitebeam, *Sorbus*, berries (**184, 185**).

185

184

186–190. In autumn some plants begin to show pathological growths or galls induced by the presence of the grubs of tiny wasps (cynipids) and flies (tephritids). Galls can be produced on any part of the plant: root, stem, leaf, flower, fruit or seed. The corky tissue of the gall protects the enclosed grubs against predators as well as the cold, rain, frost and snow. The oak tree plays host to dozens of different species of cynipid wasp, amongst them marble galls produced on leaf buds by *Andricus kollari* (**186, 187**) and knopper galls produced on acorns by *Andricus quercuscalicis* (**188**). The larvae of *A. quercuscalicis* live inside an inner, pearl-like chamber (**189**) and hatch out into females which overwinter and lay eggs asexually in the spring. Silk button spangle galls (**190**) develop on the underside of oak leaves in autumn, and are caused by *Neuroterus numismalis*. The larvae overwinter in the galls and produce a new generation in springtime.

186

187

188

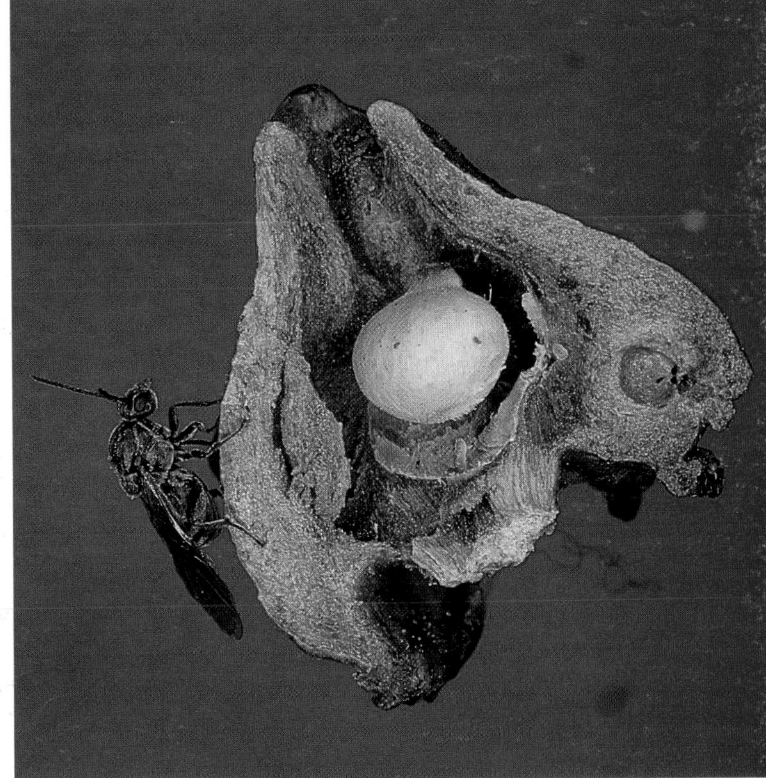

189

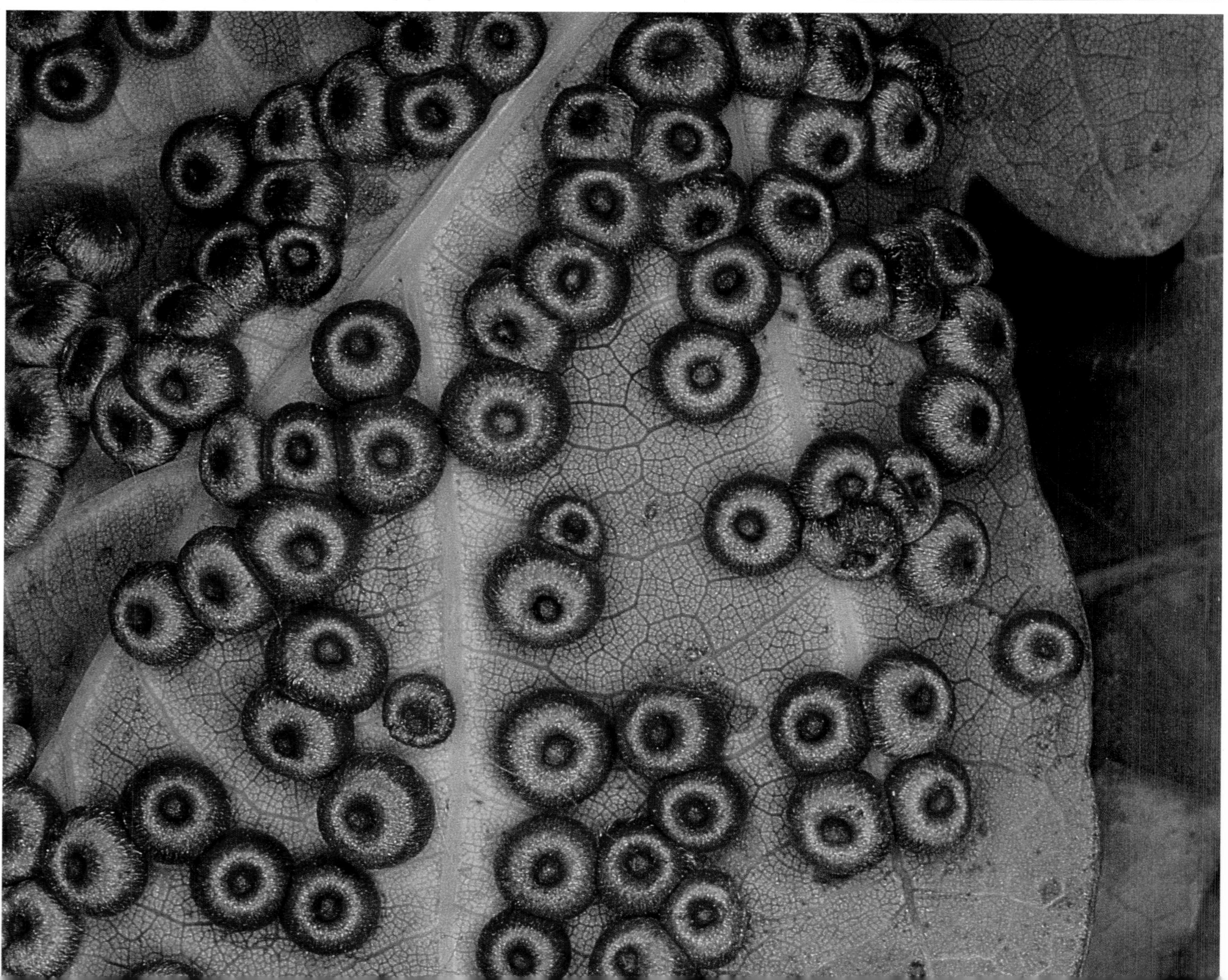

192 ▶

191–193. The same clear skies that sometimes herald an 'Indian summer' in September and October, also usher in the first ground frosts of autumn (**191**). Shrinking day-length and falling temperatures will have already forced many adult winter hibernators into their lairs, including butterflies and green lace-wings which may take refuge in our own homes (**192**). For those insects that are not prepared, the first frosts prove devastating and countless dragonflies that have tenuously hung on to life while the weather permitted now become frozen in their overnight roosts (**193**). From a strictly evolutionary point of view it must be said that these beautiful adults, or imagos, have already fulfilled their reproductive potential and are therefore expendable. The same harsh law demands that damsel-flies, stoneflies, scorpion-flies, ant-lions and the adults of most bugs (Heteroptera), moths, butterflies, grasshoppers, crickets, beetles and true flies (Diptera) will have practically disappeared *en masse* by the beginning of winter. Each species has already bequeathed to the insect community a generation in waiting, either in the form of eggs, grubs or pupae lying dormant until spring, or as larvae and nymphs that will continue to develop in winter at the bottom of ponds, streams and rivers.

193

◀ 191

194. One of the safest refuges from the winter cold, if you are an insect, is under water because no matter how far outside temperatures may plummet the deeper parts of ponds, rivers and streams will always remain unfrozen even if a layer of ice forms over the surface. Even when icicles form in the shallowest stretches of streams, as in the ford shown here, the pressure of water upstream will normally ensure that flow is maintained. Dragonflies, damsel-flies, stoneflies, caddis flies, alder flies and mayflies (none of them 'flies' in the true sense, i.e., two-winged Diptera) all owe their survival as species to the hardiness of their larvae which continue to grow and develop in streams, ponds and rivers throughout the winter months.

194

195

195–197. Dried persistent flower-heads of burdocks (**195**), thistles, knapweeds and teasels make convenient homes for a variety of over-wintering grubs of wasps, flies and moths. If you squeeze the dead heads of these plants you will often feel hard, nut-like elements. These are seeds that have been galled by flies belonging to the family Tephritidae sometimes referred to as picture-winged flies. Galls of knapweed *Centaurea* contain several chambers occupied by rather squat, pillar-like grubs of *Urophora* or *Cerajocera* (**196**). Some chambers may contain, instead of a single large grub, a number of much smaller grubs of parasitic wasps that have fed upon the fly larva. Dead heads of teasel *Dipsacus* are mined by caterpillars of the moth *Endothenia* (**197**). Teasel often grows in stands, each plant carrying twenty or more flower-heads, and not uncommonly every flower in such a stand will be found to contain its resident *Endothenia* larva. Closer inspection may also reveal that individual seeds of the flower-head are occupied by a tiny caterpillar of the moth *Cochylis* or, even more intriguingly, two or three minute grubs of a parasitic wasp that have feasted upon the *Cochylis* larva.

196

197

198

198. Pin-cushion galls of the wild rose are caused by the tiny wasp *Diplolepis rosae*. On a chill winter's day with a freezing wind cutting through the leafless and forlorn-looking hedgerows, it is hard to imagine that inside these shaggy structures numerous tiny grubs are completing their development.

199

200

199, 200. A walk beside slow-flowing streams and ditches in early springtime will reveal the stems of last year's common reed *Phragmites communis* swaying in ranks above the green shoots of this year's crop (**199**). At the ends of some of these stems will be found cigar-shaped galls in which the larva of the chloropid fly *Lipara* has spent the winter (**200**).

201 ▶

201–203. For insects small enough to squeeze inside them, hollow, dry stems of the common hogweed *Heracleum sphondylium* provide convenient winter shelter (**201**). Surprisingly, inside these frost-encrusted columns may be found scores and sometimes hundreds of living insects. Photograph **202** shows a segment of stem split down the middle to reveal a pair of tiny carabid beetles *Risophilus* nestling alongside the puparium of a tachinid fly. For the time being at least, neither is under threat from the spider *Clubiona terrestris* with which they are sharing quarters. *Risophilus* also hibernates in the dead overwintering stems of reed-mace *Typha longifolia*, nudging inside the narrow spaces between the sheathing leaf bases (**203**) along with a motley crew of similar-sized hibernators such as earwigs, small ladybirds and capsid bugs.

202

203

204. A fallen tree stump, well weathered and overgrown with a blanket of mosses, provides the setting for a unique community of winter insects. But not any old stump will suffice: it must be of a certain species, and in the right condition. The bark must be intact, and it must be thick and fissured. Oak, ash, elm and pine are ideal but the bark of sycamore, beech or hornbeam is too thin to keep the frost away from the inner wood. Insects can only get inside the stump if the bark has already been loosened and fretted by a combination of weather, fungi and micro-organisms. Felled or fallen stumps often take several years to achieve the right stage of decomposition. Some of the insects that hibernate in this particular environment are of benefit to man and it is in our interests, as well as theirs, not to be too eager to clear away fallen trees from our older woodlands.

204

205

206

207

205–207. Three immature insects regularly encountered overwinter, living just beneath rotten bark: the larva of a cardinal beetle *Pyrchroa coccinea* (**205**) which feeds on other bark insects; wood-eating leather-jackets or crane-fly larvae (**206**); and the pupa of the privet hawk moth *Sphinx ligustri* (**207**).

208, 209. The activities of wood-eating larvae, such as the leather-jackets shown in photograph **206** (on page 183), transform the area immediately beneath the bark into a friable mixture of half-digested wood and soil. This crumbly material is perfect for would-be hibernating wasps and bees which can easily scoop it out into a hollow cell. Two regular cell-hibernators are the hornet *Vespa crabro* and the bumble-bee *Bombus lucorum* shown in photographs **208** and **209** respectively. These are impregnated queens which will produce next spring's first colony of workers. The posture adopted by *Vespa* inside its hibernation cell is characteristic, its antennae being lowered over its face and wings folded lengthwise and tucked out of harm's way beneath the abdomen. Life processes have been reduced to a 'slow burn', and the overall impression is one of a reversion to the pupal state.

208

209 ▶

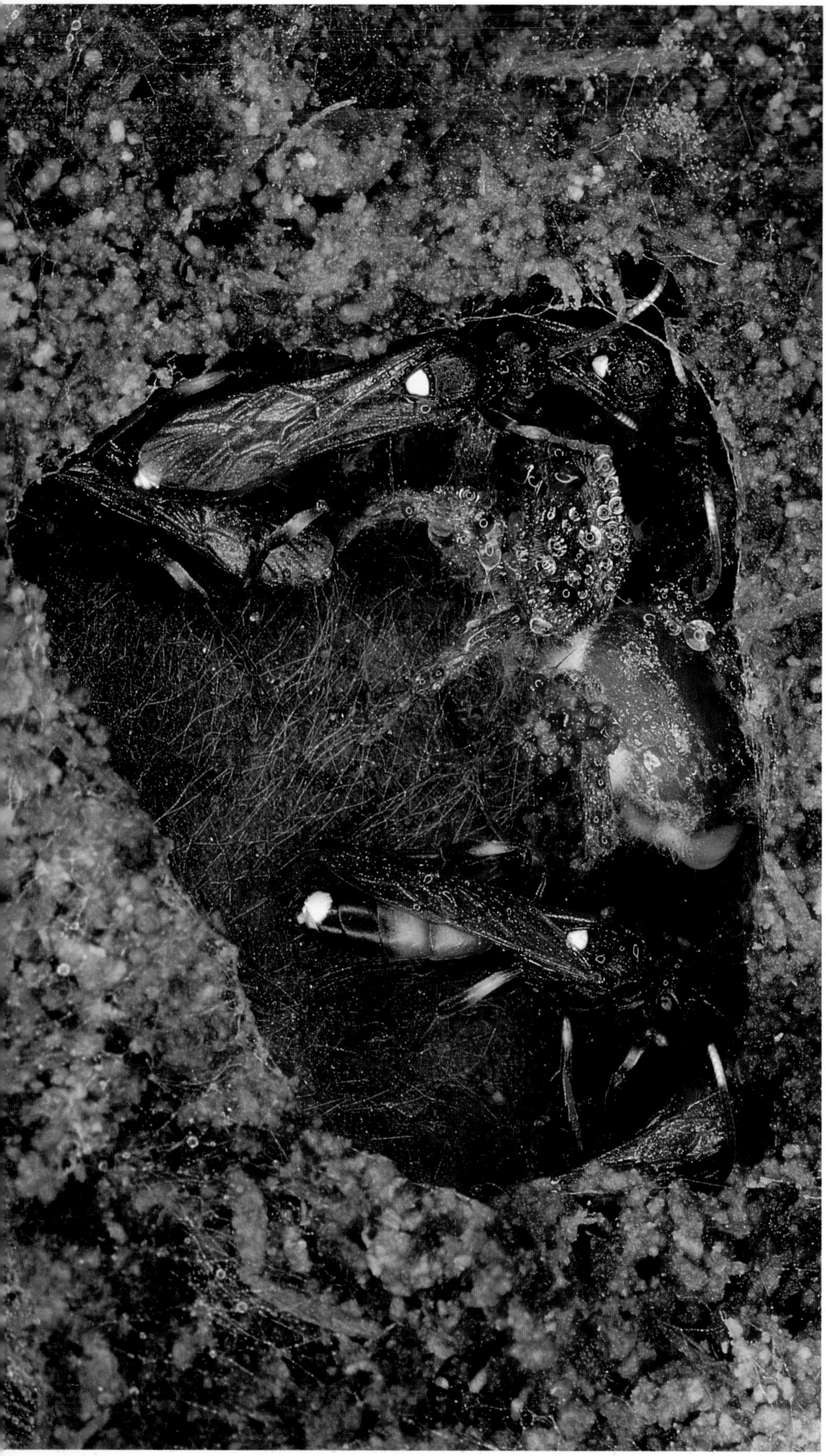

210. Adult ichneumon flies *Ichneumon suspiciosus* hibernate communally just beneath the dead bark but they are not capable of constructing their own hibernation cell. On the other hand they will occupy someone else's if the opportunity presents itself. In this particular case, a group of individuals has invaded a cell previously made by a hibernating spider which has now succumbed to fungal invasion.

210

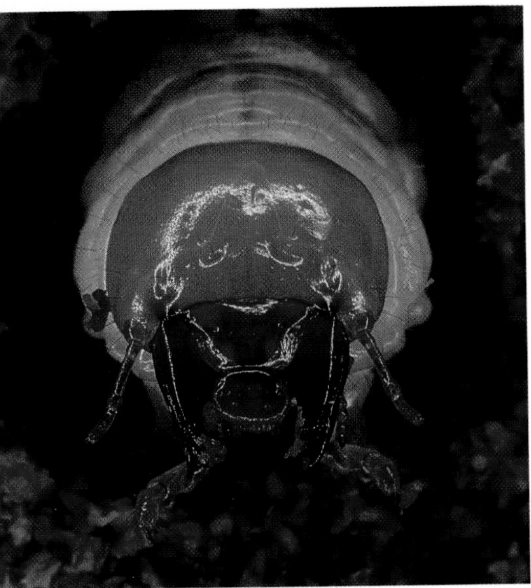

212

211, 212. The lesser stag beetle *Dorcus parallelipipedus* (**211**) hibernates deep inside the dead tree stump but, despite the impressive appearance of its jaws, it is in fact a sap-feeder and cannot chew its own way through the wood. The real wood-borer is the *Dorcus* larva (**212**) which has smaller but more powerful jaws. In its trail the larva leaves a tunnel plugged with semi-digested wood, like sawdust, which *Dorcus* senior can readily plough through to the interior of the stump.

211

213

214

213–215. The relatively dry and well-aerated conditions found beneath the bark of dead trees that remain standing (**213**) favour a different community of hibernating insects from that attracted to fallen tree stumps. Ladybirds such as *Adalia bipunctata* (**214**) and *Thea 22-punctata* (**215**) and the fungus beetle *Mycetophagus* hibernate communally in such locations, sometimes in groups of hundreds or thousands of individuals, apparently drawn together by a chemical attractant or pheromone.

215

FURTHER READING

Chapman, R. F. (1975), *Insects: Structure and Function*, London: The English Universities Press Ltd. One of the most useful general texts of entomology, covering all aspects of insect biology although lean on natural history.

Chinery, M. (1991), *Collins Guide to the Insects of Britain and Western Europe*. London: Collins. Primarily an identification manual but with good synopses of habits and lifestyles.

Imms, A. D. (1947), *Insect Natural History*. London: Collins. Now out of print, but the best account of British insect natural history yet published.

Lewington, R. & Streeter, D. (1993), *The Natural History of the Oak Tree*. Dorling Kindersley. Includes a detailed account of the extraordinary variety of insects whose lives are intertwined with that of the oak.

McGavin, G. C. (1992), *Insects of the Northern Hemisphere*. Dragon's World. Much incidental information on life cycles of all the major groups of insects.

The Collins Naturalist Handbook series is a mine of information for insect naturalists. The following are particularly relevant:

Redfern, M. & Askew, R. R. (1992), *Plant Cells*. Richmond Publishing Company Ltd.

Davis, B. N. K. (1991), *Insects on Nettles*. Richmond Publishing Company Ltd.

Unwin, D. M. & Corbet, S. A. (1991), *Insects, Plants and Microclimate*. Richmond Publishing Company Ltd.

ACKNOWLEDGEMENTS

I am greatly indebted to my wife Zena for her encouragement, support and forbearance during the period when I was collecting material for the book. Only when the question arose as to how many more days would be needed to complete the photography of the ant colony living in the wall of the house did her patience seriously begin to falter. I would also like to thank Mr Richard Wang for his untiring efforts in carrying out literature searches and for his valuable technical assistance. Mrs Jane Seymour-Shove spent many hours typing and retyping the manuscript and I am grateful for her services. Finally, I must thank Stuart Booth, the consultant editor, for his constant encouragement and for making the book possible.

INDEX

Numbers in **bold** refer to illustrations (by caption numbers)